THE PRESENT POSITION OF MINORITY
LANGUAGES IN WESTERN EUROPE

THE PRESENT POSITION OF MINORITY LANGUAGES IN WESTERN EUROPE

A Selective Bibliography

by

GLANVILLE PRICE

Professor of French, University of Stirling

CARDIFF
UNIVERSITY OF WALES PRESS
1969

Printed by Commercial & Sporting Printers Ltd.,
St. Fagan's Road, Fairwater, Cardiff

ACKNOWLEDGEMENTS

This bibliography could not have been compiled without the help of many friends and colleagues who drew my attention to items I might otherwise have missed. They are too numerous to mention individually and so I can only hope they will accept this general expression of my gratitude. I am also deeply indebted to my wife for her constant help in many respects; to the staff of the various libraries I have used in the United Kingdom, France and Switzerland and especially to those of the libraries of the Universities of St. Andrews and Stirling and the National Library of Scotland; to Judith Reid who cheerfully undertook the arduous task of typing the manuscript and helped with correcting the proofs; and to the University of Wales Press and in particular to Dr. R. Brinley Jones for his guidance and assistance.

Stirling, September 1969   G.P.

CONTENTS

I. Introduction

1. The languages covered by this bibliography are:

    (1) Basque—a non-Indo-European language spoken mainly in the Spanish provinces of Viscaya, Guipúzcoa and Navarra and also, to the north of the western Pyrenees, in the adjoining French department of Basses-Pyrénées;

    (2) Breton—the Celtic speech of western Brittany; although no reliable figures for the number of speakers are available, Breton may be the most widely-spoken of the Celtic languages;

    (3) Catalan—spoken by perhaps some 5,000,000 people mainly in Spanish Catalonia (including the Balearic Islands), but also in the Principality of Andorra (of which it is the official language), in the Roussillon in France (department of Pyrénées-Orientales) and in the town of Alghero in Sardinia;

    (4) Faroese—the language of the 30,000 inhabitants of the Faroe Islands; although the islands are administratively part of Denmark, they enjoy a considerable degree of autonomy and Faroese, which is much more closely related to Icelandic than to Danish, is now the main official language;

    (5) Frisian—by far the most widely spoken variety of the language is West Frisian, spoken by about 300,000 people in the Dutch province of Friesland and the islands of Terschelling and Schiermonnikoog; in Germany, East Frisian is spoken by a few thousand near Oldenburg in Lower Saxony, and North Frisian in parts of the west coast of Schleswig and the off-shore islands of Sylt, Föhr, Amrum and Heligoland;

    (6) Irish—the official language of the Irish Republic; according to the report on the 1961 census, the number of Irish-speakers in the Republic then numbered 716,420, but it is certain that only a small proportion of these were native speakers;

    (7) Manx—the Gaelic language of the Isle of Man; only one remaining native speaker of Manx, Mr. Ned Maddrell, was known in 1969;

    (8) Occitan—otherwise known, but less accurately, as Provençal; Provençal in the strict sense is one dialect of Occitan, the other principal varieties being Languedocien, Gascon, and various northern Occitan dialects (including Limousin, Auvergnat and Dauphinois);

    (9) Romansh—otherwise known as Raeto-Romance; it is no part of our concern to discuss whether or not the various Romansh

dialects of the Swiss canton of the Grisons (Graubünden), the non-Italian Romance dialects of the Dolomite valleys (known as Ladin) and Friulan (spoken in north-east Italy) are rightly considered to be forms of the same language; all of these dialects are grouped under Romansh in this bibliography;

(10) Sardinian;

(11) Scots, i.e. the West Germanic dialect of Scotland, otherwise known as Lallans or Lowland Scots; this is considered by some to be a dialect of English, by others to be a distinct language from English;

(12) Scottish Gaelic, spoken according to the 1961 Census by 80,978 people in Scotland, principally in the Western Isles and a few remote parts of the north-west mainland;

(13) Welsh, spoken according to the 1961 Census by 656,002 people in Wales.

2. The term 'minority languages' is not perhaps fully satisfactory, as at least two of the languages concerned, Catalan and Faroese, are still spoken by the great majority of the population of the areas with which they are traditionally associated. One can however say in justification of the term that the speakers of each language form a minority within the country or countries of which they are citizens (Denmark, France, Ireland, Italy, the Netherlands, Spain, Switzerland, the United Kingdom). The term 'regional languages' is no better and is indeed open to the further objection that Irish, Romansh, Welsh and perhaps others are in one sense or another 'national' rather than 'regional' languages. The term 'ethnic languages' (*langues ethniques*) recently adopted by some French writers is wholly inappropriate with its misleading implication of an association between language and race.

3. Languages which are spoken by a majority in one country but are at the same time minority languages in another country (e.g. Flemish, Italian and German in parts of France) fall outside the terms of reference of the present bibliography. (We exclude from this provision Catalan which, though the official language of the Principality of Andorra, is a minority language in both France and Spain.)

4. The bibliography is designed to cover such topics as the following:

(1) The number of speakers of each language;

(2) The geographical distribution of the languages;

(3) The quantitive and qualitative decline of the languages;

(4) Their official status;

(5) Their use in schools, churches, the press, etc;

(6) The problem of the creation of standard literary languages;

(7) Their present standing as literary media;

(8) Dialectal differentiation insofar as it bears on other topics listed above.

5. Items such as the following are, generally speaking, excluded:

(1) Dictionaries, works of historical or descriptive linguistics, dialectal monographs, etc.;

(2) Works of literary history or criticism;

(3) Works in languages other than English, French, German, Italian and Spanish; however, works in Catalan on Catalan and in Dutch on Frisian, and some recent works in Welsh on Welsh or another of the Celtic languages, are included;

(4) Newspaper and magazine articles, pamphlets and similar ephemera, items relating to abortive schemes of one kind or another, and works that may now be considered completely out of date; many of these will be found listed in the bibliographies referred to in Section II below.

6. Although this bibliography is concerned specifically with the present state of the languages in question, we have included in it a number of items relating to the state of one or other of the languages at various times in the past.

7. It is not, and indeed could not be, our purpose in compiling this bibliography, to offer the specialist in the field of any one of the languages treated anything that would be of particular use to him in his own speciality. Our hope is, however, that the bibliography may be of service to those who are concerned in one way or another with the fate of one or more of the languages in question and would also be interested to find out what problems are being faced by other minority languages in Western Europe and how these problems are or are not being tackled. Needless to say, the compiler is well aware that he has probably omitted a number of items that are not specifically excluded by the restrictions listed in paragraph 5 above. He can only ask those who may notice such omissions (or any errors in the present bibliography) to draw his attention to them by writing to him at the University, Stirling, Scotland, and he will at some future date include these in a supplementary list.

II. Bibliographies

Many of the bibliographies listed here cover a wider range of topics than the present bibliography. On the other hand, some aspects of the present bibliography often fall outside their scope. Other bibliographies, e.g. older ones and some that are only marginally relevant to our purposes, will be found listed under the heading of the various languages in Theodore Bestermann, *A World Bibliography of Bibliographies*, 4th edition, 5 vols., 1965-66. The annual *Bibliographie linguistique*, published by the Permanent International Committee of Linguists, is of course indispensable.

Basque:

(i) J. Vinson, *Essai d'une bibliographie de la langue basque*, [T.I.], Paris, 1891; [T.II], *Complément et supplément*, Paris, 1898.

(ii) P. Lafitte, 'La langue basque', in *Gernika-Eusko-Jakintza*, I (1947), 9-18.
[Largely devoted to a list of publications in or on Basque.]

Breton (see also **Celtic Languages**):

(i) G. von Tevenar, 'Bretonische Bibliographie', in *Zeitschrift für celtische Philologie*, 22 (1941), 77-92.

(ii) G. Berthou, 'Bretonisches Schrifttum', in *Zeitschrift für celtische Philologie*, 23 (1943), 365-388.

(iii) R. Hemon, *La langue bretonne et ses combats*, La Baule, 1947, 264 pp.; see pp. 151-250, 'Bibliographie sommaire de la langue bretonne'.
["Cette bibliographie sommaire a surtout pour but de donner une idée de ce qui a paru en breton, et dans d'autres langues au sujet du breton. Elle est loin d'être complète. Mais elle évitera de longues recherches aux lecteurs de cet ouvrage qui voudront se documenter sur tel ou tel des points étudiés."
Classified. See particularly V, 'Situation du breton', Nos. 124-142, which lists *inter alia* a number of reports on the situation of Breton published by the *Comité de préservation de la langue bretonne* between 1897 and 1917.]

(iv) B. A. Pocquet du Haut-Jussé, 'Bibliographie bretonne, années 1942-1949 et complément', in *Annales de Bretagne*, 56 (1949), 292-393 ("Langue bretonne", 351-353).
[Also lists, pp. 292-293, the previous 25 'Bibliographies bretonnes' published in the *Annales de Bretagne* between 1903 and 1942.]

Catalan:

(i) J. Amade, *Bibliographie critique pour l'étude des origines et premières manifestations de la Renaissance littéraire en Catalogne au XIXe siècle*, Toulouse-Paris, 1924, 88 pp.

(ii) R. Aramon i Serra and J. Vives, *Bibliografia de llengua i literatura catalana*, 262 pp., published in five fascicules in *Anuari de l'Oficina Romànica de lingüística i literatura*, Vols. II (1929), III (1930), IV (1931), V (1932) and VII (1934).

(iii) A. Griera, 'Le domaine catalan, compte-rendu rétrospectif jusqu'en 1924', in *Revue de linguistique romane*, I (1925), 35-113.

(iv) A. Griera, *Bibliografía lingüística catalana*, Barcelona, 1947, 84 pp.
[A revised version of (iii) above.]

(v) A. Griera, 'Les études sur la langue catalane,' in *Archivum Romanicum*, 12 (1928), 530-552.

Celtic Languages:

(i) *Bibliotheca Celtica*, National Library of Wales, Aberystwyth; annual volumes for the years 1909 to 1913 and later volumes for the years 1914-1918, 1919-1923, 1924-1926, 1927-1928.
[The arrangement is alphabetical and otherwise unclassified, which greatly reduces the utility of the bibliography.]

(ii) *Bibliotheca Celtica*, New Series; Vol. 1, 1929-1933; Vol. 2, 1934-1938; Vol. 3, 1939-1943; Vol. 4, 1944-1948; Vol. 5, 1949-1952.
[Classified according to language and subject.]

(iii) *Bibliotheca Celtica*, Third Series, annual volumes 1953- .
[Classified according to language and subject.]

Faroese:

(i) O. Werner, 'Die Erforschung der färingischen Sprache. Ein Bericht über Stand und Aufgaben', in *Orbis*, XIII (1964), 481-544; see esp. pp. 484-491, 'Die Entstehung der Schriftsprache und Sprachpflege'.

(ii) S. Amundsen, 'Bibliographie linguistique du féroïen (non compris la philologie)', in *Études Germaniques*, 20 (1965), 449-455.

Frisian:

(i) Provinciale Bibliotheek van Friesland, *Catalogus des Friesche taal- en letterkunde en overige Friesche geschriften* [voorbericht door G. A. Wumkes], Leeuwarden, 1941, xix-860 pp.

(ii) K. Fokkema's bibliographies for the following years: July, 1941-Jan. 1943, in *Frysk Jierboek*, V (1943), 9-16; 1943, in *Frysk Jierboek*, VI (1946), 9-14; 1944-1948, in *It Beaken*, X (1948), 66-78; 1948-1949, in *It Beaken*, XII (1950), 164-174; 1950-1953, in *It Beaken*, XIX (1957), 134-144 and 184; 1954, in *Friesisches Jahrbuch*, 1955, 174-179.

(iii) Y. Poortinga and H. S. Buwalda, 'Literaturübersicht, 1958-1960: Westfriesland', in *Friesisches Jahrbuch*, 1961, 269-284.

(iv) Statsbibliotek (Aarhus), *Friserne, land og folk, sprog og litteratur. Katalog*, Aarhus, 1959, 70 pp.

Irish (see **Celtic Languages**).

Manx (see also **Celtic Languages**):

W. Cubbon, *A bibliographical account of works relating to the Isle of Man*, 2 vols., London, 1933-1939.

Occitan:

(i) D. C. Haskell, *Provençal Literature and Language* . . ., A list of references in the New York Public Library, New York, 1925, 885 pp.

(ii) P.-L. Berthaud, *Bibliographie occitane, 1919-1942*, Paris, 1946, xvii-93 pp.

(iii) P.-L. Berthaud et J. Lesaffre, *Bibliographie occitane, 1943-1956*, Paris, 1958, 69 pp.

(iv) I.-M. Cluzel et J. Lesaffre, 'Bibliographie occitane, 1957-1959,' in *Revue de langue et littérature provençales*, No. 2, 2e trimestre, 1960, 87-101.

(v) I.-M. Cluzel et J. Lesaffre, *Bibliographie occitane, 1960-1961*, in *Revue de langue et littérature d'oc*, No. 9 (ler trimestre, 1962), 103-113.

(vi) I.-M. Cluzel et J. Lesaffre, 'Bibliographie occitane, 1962-1963', in *Revue de langue et littérature d'oc* (forthcoming).

(vii) Institut d'Etudes Occitanes, *Bibliografia occitana, 1960-1964*, Toulouse, 1965, 28 pp.

(viii) J. Taupiac, 'Bibliografia occitana de l'annada 1965', in *Revue des langues romanes*, 77 (1966), 189-193.

(ix) The bibliographies published annually in the *Annales du Midi*.

Romansh:

(i) M. Elizabeth Maxfield, 'Raeto-Romance Bibliography,' in *Studies in the Romance Languages and Literatures* (University of North Carolina), No. 2 (1941), 1-28.
[Lists, *inter alia*, many newspaper and magazine articles on the state of the language that are excluded from the present bibliography.]

(ii) *Bibliografia Retoromontscha, 1552-1930*, Chur, 1938, xv-266 pp.; *Bibliografia Retoromontscha, II, 1931-1952*, Chur, 1956, xi-165 pp.
[A complete alphabetical—and otherwise unclassified—list of books, pamphlets, etc. (but not articles) published in Romansh.]

Scots:

J. S. Woolley, *Bibliography for Scottish Linguistic Studies*, Edinburgh, 1954, 37 pp.
[Section II, pp. 11-20, 'Works specifically or chiefly relating to mainland Scots'.]

Scottish Gaelic (see also Celtic Languages):

J. S. Woolley, *Bibliography for Scottish Linguistic Studies*, Edinburgh, 1954, 37 pp.
[Section III (d), pp. 24-27, 'Scots Gaelic'.]

Welsh (see also Celtic Languages):

University College of Wales, Aberystwyth, Faculty of Education, *Dwyieitheg—Bilingualism: a bibliography with special reference to Wales*, 1960, 56 pp.
[Deals especially but not exclusively with Wales. Includes many works not directly concerned with bilingualism but rather with other aspects of the present state of the language. Lists numerous items that are relevant to the subject of the present bibliography but have been excluded from it as falling within one or other of the categories mentioned above, I, *Introduction*, section 5.]

III. General Works

Gen.1.   A. Dauzat, *L'Europe linguistique*, new and revised ed., Paris, 1953, 239 pp.

[Basque, pp. 32-34, 123-125, 155-156, with two maps; Breton, pp. 125-129, with a map; Catalan, pp. 57, 119, 154-155; Irish, pp. 177-178; Manx, p. 176; Occitan, pp. 55-56; Romansh, pp. 54, 159-163, with a map; Scottish Gaelic (referred to as 'Erse'), p. 176; Welsh, pp. 175-176. Not worth consulting on Faroese (considered as a dialect of Danish!—p. 192), Frisian and Sardinian.]

Gen.2.   A. Meillet, *Les langues dans l'Europe nouvelle*, 2nd ed., Paris 1928, xii-495 pp.

[The sections relevant to the present bibliography are to be found in Tesnière's Appendix, *Statistique des langues de l'Europe*, pp. 291-473; Basque, pp. 364-365, 383-384; Breton, pp. 379-382; Catalan, pp. 365, 384; Faroese, pp. 361-362; Frisian, pp. 392-393; Irish, pp. 334-336; Manx, pp. 336-337; Occitan, pp. 386-387; Romansh, pp. 351, 398-403, 428-430; Scottish Gaelic, pp. 331-334; Welsh, pp. 330-331.]

Gen.2a. J. Ventura, *Les cultures minoritàries europees*, Barcelona, 1963, 223 pp.

[In Catalan.]

Gen.3.   Department of Education and Science, *Bilingualism in Education*, London, 1965, 233 pp.

[Report on an international seminar held at Aberystwyth, Aug. Sept., 1960. Remarks *passim* on various languages covered by the present bibliography.]

IV. Basque

Ba.1.   Severo de Altube, 'La unificación del Euskera literario,' in *Eusko-Jakintza*, III (1949), 181-204.

[Suggests that the Guipuzcoan dialect should be adopted as the basis for a movement towards standardizing the literary language.]

Ba.2. Prince Lucien Bonaparte, *Carte des sept provinces basques montrant la délimitation actuelle de l'Euskara et sa division en dialectes, sous-dialectes et variétés*, London, two sheets (east and west), 1863.

[A map, scale 1/200,000, indicating the areas where Basque was spoken by a majority or by a minority of the population. Although dated 1863, the map was apparently published in reality in 1871 or 1872—see A. Dauzat, *L'Europe linguistique*, nouvelle éd., 1953, p. 124, n. 3, and R. Lafon, *Bulletin Hispanique*, 51 (1949), p. 164.]

Ba.3. P. Broca, *Sur l'origine et la répartition de la langue basque*, Paris, 1875, 54 pp. + map. (Reprinted from the *Revue d'anthropologie*.)

["Ouvrage vieilli; n'a plus d'intérêt que pour la répartition et la carte"—A. Dauzat, *L'Europe linguistique*, nouvelle éd., 1953, p. 35; the map is reproduced by G. Lacombe in his article on Basque in Meillet and Cohen's *Les langues du monde*, see below, Ba.9.]

Ba.4. Julio Caro Baroja, *Materiales para una historia de la lengua vasca en su relación con la latina*, Salamanca, 1946, 236 pp.

[See Ch.1. (pp. 7-32), 'Limites de la lengua vasca: sus dialectos y variantes', which contains a historical survey of previous works in this field.]

Ba.5. G. Fleuriot, 'La situation de la langue basque', in *La Nature*, Vol 82, No. 3231 (juillet, 1954), 270-274.

Ba.6. H. Gavel, 'Necesidad de una lengua literaria y oficial y la unificación de la ortografía vasca', in *Revue Internationale des Études Basques*, X (1919), 137-142.

Ba.7. A. Irigaray, 'Documentos para la Geografía lingüística de Navarra,' in *Revue Internationale des Études Basques*, 26 (1935), 601-623.

[On the geographical limits of Basque from the 17th century onwards.]

Ba.8. J. R. Jump, 'Basque—the Dying Language of Spain?' in *Modern Languages*, 34 (1952-53), 27-28.

[Slight].

17

Ba.9.   G. Lacombe, 'La langue basque', in A. Meillet and M. Cohen, *Les langues du monde*, nouvelle édition, Paris, 1952, pp. 257-270. [See in particular pp. 259-261 which give estimates for the numbers of Basque-speakers and discuss the geographical limits of the language and its dialects.]

Ba.10.   P. Lafitte, 'La langue basque de 1939 à 1947', in *Gernika-Eusko-Jakintza*, I (1947), 9-18.
[Discusses the attitude of the French and Spanish governments and the church to Basque; the Basque press.]

Ba.11.   R. Lafon, 'Les variations de la frontière linguistique basco-espagnole depuis le moyen-âge', in *Bulletin Hispanique*, 51 (1949) 163-169.

Ba.12.   Manuel de Lecuona, 'El Euskara en Navarra, a fines del siglo XVI,' in *Revue Internationale des Études Basques*, 24 (1933), 365-374.

Ba.13.   H. Myhill, *The Spanish Pyrenees*, London, 1966; Ch.8, 'The Dying Tongue,' pp. 90-96.
[An informal but worth-while account of a tourist's search for the last remaining Basque-speakers in the north-eastern valleys of the Province of Navarra.]

Ba.14.   N. Ormaechea, 'Unificación del lenguaje literario', in *Revue Internationale des Études Basques*, XI (1920), 53-61.

Ba.15.   Norbert Tauer, 'Baskičtina a jeji dnešni situace', in *Philologica Pragensia* (Prague), VIII (1965), 81-87.
[The Basque language and its present situation. In Czech, with a summary in Spanish.]

Ba.16.   M. Tournier, 'L'usure du basque', in *Eusko-Jakintza*, III (1949), 159-162, and IV (1950), 93-102.
[The recession of Basque in certain areas; the attitude of some Basque-speakers towards the language; the Basque periodical press.]

Ba.17.   *Journées pédagogiques pour l'enseignement du basque à l'école.* Special number of the journal *Gure Herria*, September, 1959.
[Report on a conference held at Bayonne, 27 and 28/8/1959; reproduces various papers read at the conference.]

V. Breton

Br.1.   W. Ambrose Bebb, 'Sefyllfa'r Llydaweg o'i gymharu â'r gorffenol ac o'i gymharu â Chymru,' in *Y Llenor*, 4 (1925), 113-128.
[In Welsh: 'The situation of Breton compared with the past and compared with Wales'.]

Br.2.   A. Dauzat, 'Le déplacement des frontières linguistiques: le recul des dialectes celtiques, principalement en Bretagne', in *Studies ... presented to John Orr*, Manchester, 1953, 34-44.

Br.3.   A. Dauzat, 'La pénétration du français en Bretagne du XVIIIe siècle à nos jours', in *Revue de philologie française*, XLI (1929), 1-55. Reprinted under the title 'La diffusion du français en Bretagne du XVIIIe siècle à nos jours' in Dauzat's *Études de linguistique française*, 2e éd., Paris, 1946, 101-145.

Br.4.   A. Dauzat, 'Le breton et le français', in *La Nature*, 54e année, No. 2717, mai, 1926, 273-278.
[See also No. 21 below.]

Br.5.   Per Denez, *Au sujet de l'orthographe bretonne*, [Buhulien], 1958, 38 pp. (cyclostyled).
[The case against Falc'hun's orthographic proposals (see Nos. 8 and 10 below).]

Br.6.   Alain Du Scorff, 'Le breton, langue vivante', in *Mercure de France*, No. 658, 15-xi-1925, 88-110.
[An account of the hostility or indifference to Breton shown by the civil and ecclesiastical authorities and by many Breton-speakers themselves, and a plea for a modest place for the teaching of Breton in schools.]

Br.7.   E. Ernault, *Le breton et l'enseignement*, S. Brieuc, 1928.

Br.8.   F. Falc'hun, 'Autour de l'orthographe bretonne', in *Annales de Bretagne*, LX (1953), 48-77.
[Historical account of the attempts to create a standardized spelling, and a discussion of the problems involved, in view of the existence of profound dialectal differences.]

Br.9.   F. Falc'hun, 'Langue bretonne', in *Orbis*, VII (1958), 516-533.
[Historical considerations; dialects; present situation.]

Br.10.   F. Falc'hun, *L'orthographe universitaire de la langue bretonne*,
Brest, [1956], 38 pp.
[A statement of the need for and conditions of a reform of
Breton orthography, and an exposition of the proposed system.
A preface, 'Les vicissitudes de l'orthographe bretonne', by
L. Dujardin, traces the history of the problem with particular
reference to the period from 1941 onwards. For an opposing
view, see No. 5 above.]

Br.11.   F. Falc'hun et P. Trépos, *La langue bretonne et l'enseignement*,
(Rapports présentés à la Journée Culturelle Bretonne, Rennes,
26-4-52), [1952], 31 pp.
[Falc'hun, 'La langue bretonne et les études celtiques dans
l'enseignement supérieur en France', pp. 1-12; Trépos, 'La langue
bretonne et l'enseignement secondaire', pp. 13-31.]

Br.12.   [Yann Fouéré], *Enseigner le breton, exigence bretonne*, Rennes,
1938, 59 pp.

Br.13.   [Yann Fouéré], *Nous devons obtenir l'enseignement du breton*,
Rennes, 1935, 31 pp.

Br.14.   M. Gautier, *La Bretagne centrale*, La Roche-sur-Yon, 1947, 453
pp.
[Pp. 313-314, the linguistic boundary in central Brittany in
1946, commune by commune, map and commentary.]

Br.15.   F. Gourvil, *Langue et littérature bretonnes*, Paris, 1952, 128 pp.
[Pp. 96-105, Les dialectes; pp. 105-109, Situation actuelle de la
langue bretonne.]

Br.16.   M. Guieysse, *La langue bretonne, ce qu'elle fut, ce qu'elle est, ce
qui se fait pour elle et contre elle*, Quimper, 1936, 271 pp.
[See particularly Ch. IV, 'La langue bretonne, les autorités
religieuses et les partis', pp. 135-164; Ch. V, 'La langue bretonne
et les pouvoirs publics', pp. 165-201; Ch. VI, 'Le mouvement
contemporain', pp. 202-251; 'Conclusion', pp. 251-257.]

Br.17.   R. Hemon, *La langue bretonne et ses combats*, La Baule, 1947, 261 pp.

Br.18.   R. Hemon, 'Die Vereinheitlichung des Bretonischen,' in *Zeitschrift für celtische Philologie*, 22 (1941), 293-306; with an *Anhang*, ibid., 23 (1943), 121-124.

Br.19.   H. Ll. Humphreys, *Étude socio-linguistique sur la pénétration de la langue française en Bretagne, avec une étude spéciale de la situation linguistique autour de la ligne Uzel-Saint-Nicholas-du-Pelem (Côtes du Nord)*.
[Thesis in preparation for the degree of M.A. of the University of Wales.]

Br.19a. P. Kéraval, 'Quelques aspects de la géographie linguistique en Cornouaille', in *Pen ar Bed*, Nouvelle série, No. 2 (janvier, 1954), 9-10, and No. 3 (avril, 1954), 5-6.
[An account of distributions and trends.]

Br.20.   Alfred Le Quer, 'Le recul du breton aux alentours de Questembert', in *Annales de Bretagne*, 59 (1952), 265-267.
[A map and a brief accompanying note.]

Br.21.   J. Loth, 'Les langues bretonne et française en Bretagne d'après un travail récent', in *Revue Celtique*, 43 (1926), 419-427.
[Takes up and corrects various sections of Dauzat's article in *La Nature*, No. 4 above.]

Br.22.   J. Martray, *Le problème breton et la réforme de la France*, La Baule, 1947, 223 pp.
[The following chapters deal with the language: I, iii, 'Le miracle breton aux XIXe et XXe siècles', pp. 47-67; III, ii, 'Nos droits méconnus', pp. 105-116.]

Br.23.   P. Mocaer, 'The Breton Language', in *The Celtic Conference, 1917: Reports*, Perth, 1919, 77-83.
[The state of the Breton language.]

Br.24.   [Jean] Ogée, *Dictionnaire historique et géographique de la province de Bretagne*, nouvelle édition revue et augmentée par MM. A. Marteville et P. Varin, Rennes, 2 vols., 1843-1853.
[The interest of this gazetteer for our purposes is that, for each

locality, a linguistic comment is made, generally "On parle le breton", "On parle le français" or "On parle le breton et le français", but occasionally something more extensive, such as, for Locminé, "On parle généralement le français dans la ville et le breton dans la partie rurale", or, for Lennon, "On parle beaucoup plus généralement le breton que le français". These comments are not included in Ogée's original edition of the work (Nantes, 4 vols., 1778-80).

My attention was drawn to this work by Mr. D. M. Lloyd, Keeper of Printed Books at the National Library of Scotland, Edinburgh, who intends to publish a map showing the distribution of Breton and French in Brittany on the basis of the indications given in the gazetteer.]

Br.25.　R. Panier, 'Les limites actuelles de la langue bretonne: leur évolution depuis 1886' in *Le français moderne*, X (1942), 97-115.
[Changes in the linguistic border since Sébillot's investigation, see No. 28 below.]

Br.26.　H. Rheinfelder, 'Brief aus der Bretagne', in *Im Dienste der Sprache: Festschrift für V. Klemperer*, Halle, 1958, pp. 336-349.
[Observations on the present state of Breton.]

Br.27.　P. Sébillot, 'La statistique de la langue bretonne', in *Revue Celtique*, 4 (1879-80), 128-130.
[Estimates the number of monoglot Breton-speakers to be some 705,500; methodologically dubious.]

Br.28.　P. Sébillot, 'La langue bretonne, limites et statistiques', in *Revue d'Ethnographie*, V (1886), 1-29.

Br.29.　G. von Tevenar, 'Die Zeitschrift *Gwalarn* und die neuere Sprachbewegung in der Bretagne', in *Zeitschrift für celtische Philologie*, XXII (1941), 215-238.
[Surveys, *inter alia*, the pre-war campaign in favour of the teaching of Breton in state and church schools.]

Br.30.　F. Vallée, 'Some notes on the situation of the Breton language, in Brittany', in *Transactions of the Celtic Congress, 1918*, Swansea 1918, 108-111.
[The unsuccessful attempts to have Breton taught in schools; the state of the Breton press.]

Br.31.   H. Zimmer, 'Die keltische Bewegung in der Bretagne', in *Preussische Jahrbücher*, 99 (1900), 454-497.

Br.32.   'La prédication et le catéchisme en langue bretonne', in *Revue celtique*, 47 (1930), 249-250.
[Note on a survey carried out by the Breton-language journal *Gwalarn* in 1928.]

Br.32a. 'Rapport du Comité de préservation de la langue bretonne', in *Bulletin . . . de l'Association Bretonne*, 4e série, t. 49 (1938) xvii-xlii.

Br.33.   'Rapport sur la situation faite actuellement à la langue bretonne dans l'enseignement, l'administration, la radiotélévision,' présenté par la délégation bretonne au congrès de l'U.F.C.E. (Bruges, mai 1961). (Supplément à *L'Avenir*, juin, 1961; also inserted as a supplement in *Skol*, No. 21, May, 1963.)

Br.34.   The periodical *Le Peuple Breton* records various post-war moves to have the teaching of Breton authorized in schools in the following numbers: 1 (Oct. 1947), pp. 3-5; 7 (April, 1948), p. 4; 9 (June, 1948), p. 11; 11 (Sept. 1948), p. 3.

VI. Catalan

Cat.1.   J. Amade, *Origines et premières manifestations de la Renaissance littéraire en Catalogne au XIXe siècle*, Toulouse-Paris, 1924, 568 pp.

Cat.2.   R. Aramon i Serra, 'L'Institut d'Études Catalanes et son activité linguistique', in *Communications et Rapports du Premier Congrès International de Dialectologie Générale*, IVe partie, Louvain, 1965, 7-20.

Cat.3.   A. M. Badia i Margarit, *Llengua i cultura als països catalans*, Barcelona, 1964, 197 pp.
[See especially the following chapters:
El cinquantenari de les normes ortogràfiques, pp. 79-96; *El català des de Pompeu Fabra fins a Carles Riba*, 97-104; *Tres problemes del català d'avui*, 105-116 (the three problems discussed are (i)

the insufficient means of teaching and fostering the language, (ii) mass immigration of non-Catalans into Catalonia, (iii) the gap between the literary language and the spoken language); *La joventut, de cara a dues cultures*, 119-133; *El bilingüisme català-castellà*, 135-147.]

Cat.4. A. Badía Margarit, *Gramática catalana*, Madrid, 2 vols., 1962. [See I, 11-44: observations on the geographical and numerical extension of Catalan, dialects, codification of the language, work of the Institut d'Estudis Catalans, etc.]

Cat.5. A. Badía Margarit, *Gramática histórica catalana*, Barcelona, 1951, 385 pp. [See pp. 50-63 'Extensión y vitalidad del catalan' (with four maps); pp. 65-80 'Lengua y dialectos'.]

Cat.6. A. Badía Margarit, 'Some aspects of bilingualism amongst cultured people in Catalonia,' in *Proceedings of the Ninth International Congress of Linguists* (Cambridge, Mass., 1962), The Hague, 1964, 366-373.

Cat.7. B. Banqué, 'La llengua catalana i el franquisme,' in *Beiträge zur romanischen Philologie*, II (1963), Heft 2, 111-124.

Cat.8. R. Brummer, 'L'importance de la prose dans la formation de la langue littéraire catalane,' in *VIII Congresso internazionale di Studi romanzi* (Firenze, 1956), Atti, II, Florence, 1960, 91-96.

Cat.9. A. Brun, *L'introduction de la langue française en Béarn et en Roussillon*, Paris, 1923, 94 pp.

Cat.10. Joan Coromines, *El que s'ha de saber de la llengua catalana*, Palma de Mallorca, 1954, 145 pp. [See especially 'Limits i gent que la parla', pp. 9-16; 'Antecedents històrics', pp. 27-36; 'Els dialectes catalans. La unificació i normalització de la llengua literària', pp. 56-66.]

Cat.11. A. Griera, *La frontera catalano-aragonesa, estudi geografico-lingüístic*, Barcelona, 1914, 124 pp.

Cat.12. E. Guiter, 'La llengua literària del Rosselló en aquest darrer segle,' in *VIII Congresso internazionale di Studi romanzi* (Firenze, 1956), Atti, II, Florence, 1960, 173-197.

Cat.13. M. de Montoliu, *La llengua literària*, Sabadell, 1933, 30 pp.

Cat.14. G. Normandy, *La question catalane*, Paris, 1908, 112 pp.
[Ch. II, 'La Renaissance catalane,' pp. 9-20.]

Cat.15. L. Pastre, 'Le catalan à l'école,' in *Revue catalane*, I (1907), 21-25, 46-53, 78-83.
[This article by the Secretary of the *Société d'Études Catalanes* is interesting as an illustration of a certain state of mind: the author is *opposed* to the teaching of Catalan in schools as a subject in its own right, but advocates that it *should* be used in schools as an aid to teaching French; his Society should however, by competitions and prizes, encourage children to study Catalan *outside* school.]

Cat.16. C. C. Rice, 'Notes on the present status of the Catalan language', in *Modern Language Forum*, XIII (1928), 22; reprinted in the posthumous collection of Rice's articles, *Romance Etymologies and other Studies*, Chapel Hill, 1946, 97-98.

Cat.17. Earl W. Thomas, 'The Resurgence of Catalan,' in *Hispania*, XLV (1962), 43-48.

Cat.18. Ph. Torreilles, 'La diffusion du français à Perpignan après l'annexion (1660-1700)', in *Bulletin de la Société agricole, scientifique et littéraire des Pyrénées-Orientales*, 55 (1914), 365-381.

Cat.18a. F. Vallverdú, *L'escriptor català i el problema de la llengua*, Barcelona, 1968, 191 pp.
['The Catalan writer and the problem of the language'. Discusses *inter alia* the problems of the economics of Catalan publishing, bilingualism, the teaching of Catalan, the use of Catalan in books, periodicals, the theatre and public speaking, radio, television, etc., linguistic norms.]

Cat.18b. J. Veny i Clar, 'Situació de la llengua catalana', in *Un segle de vida catalana*, Vol. 1, Barcelona, 1961, pp. 71-82.

Cat.19. 'Estadística de la llengua catalana per a l'any 1930', in *Butlletí de dialectologia catalana*, XX (1932), 5-11.
[Estimates the number of speakers at *c.* 5,000,000, including *c.* 200,000 in France.]

Cat.20. *Primer Congrés de la llengua catalana*, Barcelona, 1908, 701 pp.
[Papers read at the 1906 congress, some of them dealing with various aspects of the situation of the language at the time.]

Cat.21. *Europe* (revue mensuelle, Paris), 45e année, No. 464, décembre, 1967, *Littérature catalane*.
[The following articles are particularly relevant to the subject of the present bibliography: F. Vallverdu 'L'édition catalane actuelle,' pp. 38-45; A. Blanes, 'Le théâtre catalan de ces vingt-cinq dernières années', pp. 173-182; relevant details are also included in M. Tourné's *Chronologie catalane* [1939-1966], pp. 207-222, and other articles.]

VII. Celtic Languages (general)

Celt.1. R. Hindley, *The Distribution of the Gaelic Languages since 1800: a study in linguistic geography*.
[Thesis in preparation for the degree of Ph.D. of the University of Leeds.]

Celt.2. Emrys Jones, 'The Changing Distribution of the Celtic Languages in the British Isles', in *Transactions of the Honourable Society of Cymmrodorion*, 1967, 22-38.

Celt.3. G. Price, 'The Celtic Languages in the light of some recent reports'.
[Article in preparation.]

Celt.4. E. G. Ravenstein, 'On the Celtic Languages in the British Isles', in *Journal of the Royal Statistical Society*, 42 (1879), 579-636.
["An inquiry into the geographical distribution and numerical strength of the non-English speaking inhabitants of the British Isles". N.B. this report was produced before questions relating to Scottish Gaelic and Welsh were included on the census schedule, though a question relating to Irish had been included

since 1851. See Ireland, pp. 581-591 and 624-635, with two maps, based on census reports; Isle of Man, pp. 591-592, based on Jenner's survey; Scotland, pp. 592-607, with a map; Wales, pp. 608-622. Ravenstein's article is the basis for Sébillot's brief statistical survey, 'Les langues celtiques dans les Iles Britanniques et en France', in *Revue Celtique*, IV (1879-80), 277-278.]

Celt.5. W. H. Rees, *Le bilinguisme des pays celtiques*, Rennes, 1939, 252 pp.

Celt.6. M. L. Sjoestedt-Jonval, 'Les langues de culture en celtique', in *Conférences de l'Institut de Linguistique de l'Université de Paris*, VI (1938), 59-87.

Celt.7. Derick S. Thomson, 'The Role of the Writer in a Minority Culture', in *Transactions of the Gaelic Society of Inverness*, XLIV (1967).
[Deals specifically with the Celtic languages and in particular with Scottish Gaelic.]

Celt.8. H. Zimmer, 'Der Pan-Keltismus im Großbritannien und Irland. Teil I: Die heutige nationale Bewegung in Wales in ihrer geschichtlichen Entwicklung; Teil II: Die sprachlich-literarische Bewegung in Irland und ihre Aussichten; Teil III: Das Wiederaufleben des Keltentums in seinen Folgen für England', in *Preussische Jahrbücher*, 92 (1898), 426-494; 93 (1898), 59-93, 294-334.

Celt.9. Kendalc'h Keltiek Etrevroadel: International Celtic Congress, Landreger, 1962. *Danevellskridoù: Transactions*, 168 pp.
[Contains papers—with an English translation if the original is not in English—on the position of the Celtic languages in education and publishing, on modern literature in the Celtic languages, on the social and official position of the Celtic languages, on movements working for the Celtic languages.]

Celt.10. *Maintaining a National Identity*, Dublin, 1968, 168 pp. (Celtic League 1968 Annual).
[Contains, *inter alia*, a number of papers on aspects of the present situation of the various Celtic languages.]

VIII. Faroese

Far.1.   S. Amundsen, 'Le féroïen', in *Études Germaniques*, XVIII (1963), 344-352.
[Historical survey of the fortunes of the language and the creation of literary standards.]

Far.2.   H. Kloss, *Die Entwicklung neuer germanischer Kultursprachen von 1800 bis 1950*, Munich, 1952, pp. 87-91.

Far.3.   E. Krenn, *Föroyische Sprachlehre*, Heidelberg, 1940, 139 pp.
[The introduction gives a historical survey of the establishment of the modern literary language.]

Far.4.   W. B. Lockwood, 'Literary Language and Dialect in Faroese', in *Archivum Linguisticum*, VIII (1956), 129-134.

Far.5.   W. B. Lockwood, 'Notes on the Faroese Language Today', in *Transactions of the Philological Society*, 1950, 88-111.

Far.6.   O. Werner, 'Die Erforschung der färingischen Sprache. Ein Bericht über Stand und Aufgaben,' in *Orbis*, XIII (1964), 481-544.
[A bibliographical survey; see especially pp. 484-491, 'Die Entstehung der Schriftsprache und Sprachpflege.']

Far.7.   Karel Zeman, 'Zur Entstehung der föröyischen (faröischen) Schrift- und Literatur-Sprache,' in *Sborník Vysoké Školy Pedagogické v Olomouci, Jazyk a Literatura* (Prague), VI (1959), 45-53.

IX. France (general)

Fra.1.   J. Aurouze, *La pédagogie régionaliste (les parlers locaux dans l'enseignement)*, Avignon, 1907, xiv-217 pp.

Fra.2.   F. Brunot, *Histoire de la langue française*, T. VII, *La propagation du français en France jusqu'à la fin de l'ancien régime*, Paris, 1926, 360 pp.
[See especially the following chapters:
Livre Ier, 'La vie intellectuelle et morale', Ch. III, 'Disparition de la littérature en patois' (in the Occitan-speaking area), pp. 21-24;

Livre IV, 'Le français dans les provinces particularistes ou de langue hétérogène', Ch. I, 'Béarn et Pays basque', pp. 233-237; Ch.II, 'Roussillon', pp. 238-244; Ch. IV, 'Bretagne', pp. 249-267; Livre V, 'Quelques renseignements sur l'état linguistique à la fin de l'ancien régime', Ch. II 'Le français en pays de langue d'oc et sur les confins', pp. 305-313; Ch. IV, 'Le bilinguisme', pp. 319-320 (deals especially with the Occitan-speaking area).]

Fra.3.   F. Brunot, 'Limite de la langue française sous le premier empire', in *Histoire de la langue française*, T. IX, première partie, 1927, pp. 525-599.
[Based on an official investigation of 1806; plots with numerous maps the zones of contact between French (or Occitan) and Basque, Breton, Flemish, German and Italian; Brunot's account of Breton is the subject of a note in the *Revue celtique*, 44 (1927), 239-241.]

Fra.4.   A. Dauzat, 'Le déplacement des frontières linguistiques du français de 1806 à nos jours', in *La Nature*, 55 (1927), 529-535.

Fra.5.   H. Gavel, 'Sobre la enseñanza de las lenguas regionales', in *Revue Internationale des Études Basques*, XV (1924), 610-627.
[In Spanish, but relates mainly to France.]

Fra.6.   R. Lafont, *Sur la France*, Paris, 1968, 263 pp.
[Considers the problem of minority languages within the framework of the general problem of regionalism versus centralism in France and of broader issues. The author's earlier book, *La révolution régionaliste*, Paris, 1967, 250 pp., is concerned only in passing with the problem of regional languages, but serves to put this problem into its wider context.]

Fra.7.   Michel Legris, 'Les "parlers maternels" en France', a series of nine articles published in *Le Monde*, 9-18 sept., 1964, and reprinted in *Noutro Dzen Patoué* (Aosta), No. 4, 1966, 15-51.
[A Catalan translation by Joan Cornudella Barberà appeared in book form under the title *Les parles maternes*, Barcelona, 1965, 66 pp.]

Fra.8.   A. Perbosc, *Les langues de France à l'école*, Toulouse, 1926, 54 pp.
[Reprints various articles; interesting for the history of efforts to have the teaching of regional languages authorized in state schools.]

Fra.9. P. Sérant, *La France des Minorités*, Paris, 1965, 412 pp.

[A clear, well-informed and untendentious account of the linguistic minorities in France and their cultural, political and economic problems.]

Fra.10. The text of the law of 11 Jan. 1951 authorizing a strictly limited amount of teaching of local languages in state schools (the so-called *loi Deixonne*) is to be found in the *Journal Officiel de la République Française: Lois et Décrets*, for 13 January, 1951, p. 483.

[Under nos. 11-16 below, we list various articles, including some newspaper articles, published during the progress of the bill through the French parliament or after it became law.]

Fra.11. A. Dauzat, 'Le dialecte à l'école', in *Le français moderne*, 18 (1950), 161-162.

[On the failure of an attempt to get a law allowing the teaching of local languages passed by the French parliament. See also *ibid.*, pp. 292-300, various documents relating to the *projet de loi* in question.]

Fra.12. A. Dauzat, (i) 'Le français et le dialecte à l'école', in *Le Monde*, 15-3-1950; (ii) 'Le dialecte à l'école: autour d'un projet de loi', *ibid.*, 29-3-1950; (iii) 'Ce qu'on peut faire pour les dialectes', *ibid.*, 4-10-1950.

[Dauzat opposes the teaching of regional languages in state schools.]

Fra.13. G. Duhamel, (i) 'Un attentat contre l'unité française,' in *Le Figaro*, 29/30-4-1950; (ii) 'La Tour de Babel', *ibid.*, 5-5-1950; (iii) 'Pour les contradicteurs de bonne foi', *ibid.*, 12-5-1950; (iv) 'Bilan d'une controverse', *ibid.*, 19-5-1950.

[A series of articles expressing the author's hostility to the teaching of regional languages in schools. Duhamel returns to the subject in his weekly column 'D'un samedi à l'autre' in *France-Illustration* 13-5-1950.]

Fra.14. Max Rouquette, articles on the 'projet de loi Deixonne' in *Annales de l'Institut d'Études Occitanes*, II (1950), 49-57 and 111.

Fra.15. P.-L. Berthaud, 'La loi relative à l'enseignement des langues et dialectes locaux', in *Lo Gai Saber*, No. 237, Jan.-Feb., 1951, 243-255.

[An account of the progress of the bill through both houses of the French parliament and of the modifications it underwent in the process.]

Fra.16. J. Lesaffre, 'Autour de la loi Deixonne. Le point de vue de l'adversaire', in *Lo Gai Saber*, No. 242, Nov.-Dec., 1951, 361-373; No. 243, Jan.-Feb., 1952, 405-412.

[An objective exposé, by one who does not share them, of the arguments advanced in parliament and the press against the teaching of regional languages in schools.]

Fra.17. 'L'enseignement de la langue d'oc devant l'Assemblée nationale', in *Revue de Langue et Littérature Provençales*, No. 2, 2e trimestre 1960, 58-86.

[The texts, with commentary, of three proposed bills tabled in the French parliament in 1959-1960 with a view to improving the status of regional languages in state schools. The text of a further proposal, which would take account of all three of those referred to above, is given in the *Revue de Langue et Littérature Provençales*, No. 7-8, 3e et 4e trimestres, 1961, 147-149.]

Fra.18. *Les langues de France et l'école publique* (Cahier No. 1 du Mouvement Laïque des Cultures Régionales), Nîmes-Brest, 1959, 24 pp.

Fra.19. *Pour un statut de l'enseignement des langues régionales* (Cahier No. 2 du Mouvement Laïque des Cultures Régionales), Nîmes-Brest, 1960, 24 pp.

Fra.20. *Les langues régionales de France et l'école publique* (Cahier No. 3 du Mouvement Laïque des Cultures Régionales), Nîmes-Brest, 1960, 8 pp.

X. Frisian

Fri.1. Krine Boelens, (a) 'De taalsituatie in de Stellingwerven', in *Driemaandelijkse Bladen*, VIII (1956), 81-90, with a map, (b) 'De taalsituatie in het Westerkwartier van Groningen,' *ibid.*, 151-155, with a map.
[The linguistic situation in (a) south-west Friesland, (b) the western part of the province of Groningen.]

Fri.2. K. Boelens & J. v. d. Veen, *De taal van het schoolkind in Friesland*, Leeuwarden, 1956, 132 pp.
[The results of a survey of the language of schoolchildren in Friesland.]

Fri.3. K. Fokkema, 'Hoe de Friezen spreken', in *Encyclopedie van Friesland*, Amsterdam and Brussels, 1958, 40-50.
[Contains maps of the West, East and North Friesian-speaking areas (p.43) and of the dialectal areas within West Frisian (p. 45).]

Fri.4. K. Fokkema, *De Invloed van het Stadsfries op het Fries*, in the collective volume *De Invloed van het Stadsfriesch op het Friesch* (Bijdragen en Mededeelingen der Dialecten-Commissie van de Nederlandsche Akademie van Wetenschappen te Amsterdam, IV, 1943) pp. 1-10.
[The influence of urban Frisian on Frisian.]

Fri.5. K. Fokkema, *Over de groei van het Friese taalbesef*, Groningen, 1949, 28 pp.
[The growth of Frisian linguistic awareness.]

Fri.6. K. Fokkema, *Het Stadsfries: Een bijdrage tot de geschiedenis en de grammatica van het dialect van Leeuwarden*, Assen, 1937, 186 pp.
[See pp. 4-74, *De oorzaken van het terugdringen van het Fries in Leeuwarden* ('The causes of the recession of Frisian in Leeuwarden'), a historical survey.]

Fri.7. K. Fokkema, 'Taalverhoudingen in Leeuwarden', in *Taal en Tongval* (Bosvoorde, Belgium), XII (1960), 24-33.
[The linguistic situation in Leeuwarden.]

Fri.8. K. Fokkema, 'Het Westfries en het Stadsfries in het defensif', in *Westfriesch Jaarboek*, V (1943), 10-24.
[West Frisian and urban Frisian on the defensive.]

Fri.9. Y. Foppema, *Het Fries in Nederland*, Drachten, 1952.
[A revised version of a lecture, *Het Fries en de Friese letterkunde in Nederland*, published in *Jaarboek van de Maatschappij der Nederlandse Letterkunde te Leiden*, 1947-49, 36-58.]

Fri.10. K. Heeroma, 'Die Grenze des Friesischen', in *Festschrift für Ludwig Wolff*, Neumünster, 1962, 33-53, with three maps.
[The limits of Frisian in the Netherlands as revealed by a study of isoglosses.]

Fri.11. W. G. Hellinga, 'Het Stadsfries en de problemen van taalverhoudingen en taalinvloed', in *Tijdschrift voor Nederlandse Taal- en Letterkunde*, 59 (1940), 19-52 and 125-158.
[Urban Frisian and the problems of linguistic relationships and linguistic influence.]

Fri.12. H. Kloss, *Die Entwicklung neuer germanischer Kultursprachen von 1800 bis 1950*, Munich, 1952, pp. 63-69.

Fri.13. P. Kollmann, 'Der Umfang des friesischen Sprachgebiets im Grossherzogtum Oldenburg', in *Zeitschrift des Vereins für Volkskunde*, I (1891), 377-403.

Fri.14. W. Krogmann, 'Das Schicksal der ostfriesischen Sprache', in *Jahrbuch der Gesellschaft für bildende Kunst und vaterländische Altertümer zu Emden*, 36 (1956), 97-112.

Fri.15. W. B. Lockwood, *An Informal History of the German Language*, Cambridge, 1965 (Ch. 12, 'Frisian', pp. 214-234.)
[Includes a map showing the various Frisian-speaking areas.]

Fri.16. P. Post, *Bilinguisme in Nederland. Een beschouwing over de wenselijkheid van een Fries-Nederlandse school in Friesland*, Paedagogische Monographieën, I, Groningen, 1949, 40 pp.
[Bilingualism in the Netherlands; a consideration of the desirability of a Frisian-Dutch school in Friesland.]

Fri.17. T. Siebs, 'Geschichte der friesischen Sprache', in H. Paul, *Grundriss der germanischen Philologie*, 2nd ed., Strasbourg, 1901, pp. 1152-1464.

[See especially pp. 1152-1176, 'Einleitung. Begriff und Stellung der friesischen Sprache', which includes, *inter alia*, an account of the numerical and geographical extent of the various dialects at various periods. N.B. in the first edition of Paul's *Grundriss*, Vol. I, 1891, the *Einleitung* to Siebs's section on Frisian runs to only 3 pages, pp. 723-726.]

Fri.18. G. van der Woude, 'Standaardtaal en dialekt in Friesland', in *Taal en Tongval*, XII (1960), 9-23, with a map.

[Standard language and dialect in Frisian.]

XI. Irish

Ir.1. C. Anderson, *Historical Sketches of the Native Irish and their Descendants*, 2nd edition, enlarged, Edinburgh, 1830, 358 pp. (First edition, 1828).

[Section V, 'The Irish Language and its extent', pp. 206-231, gives a well-documented account of the extent to which the language was spoken in various parts of Ireland before the Famine.]

Ir.1a. R. A. Breatnach, 'Characteristics of Irish dialects in process of extinction,' in *Communications et rapports du Premier Congrès International de Dialectologie générale* (1960), Louvain, 1964, 2 vols., I, 141-145.

[The influence of English on Irish vocabulary and syntax.]

Ir.2. R. A. Breatnach, 'Revival or Survival? An examination of the Irish language policy of the state', in *Studies*, 45 (1956), 129-145.

[A reasoned criticism of official language policy, the result of which has been to "put into currency in the schools a travesty of Irish".]

Ir.3. E. Cahill, 'Irish Language and Tradition (1540-1691)', in *Irish Ecclesiastical Record*, 54 (1939), 123-142.

[Though banished from official and educational life, Irish continued to be spoken in its purity by practically all classes of the population.]

Ir.3a   E. Cahill, 'The Irish Language in the Penal Era', in *Irish Ecclesiastical Record*, 55 (1940), 591-617.

Ir.3b.   T. P. Coogan, *Ireland Since the Rising*, London, 1966, xii-355pp.
         [Chapter 9, 'Gaelic Movement', pp. 183-205, gives an historical survey and an account of the present state of the language and the problems of its revival.]

Ir.4.   D. Corkery, *The Fortunes of the Irish Language*, Dublin, 1954, 129 pp.
         [The history of Irish from the earliest times, period by period.]

Ir.4a.   E. Curtis, 'The spoken languages of medieval Ireland', in *Studies*, 8 (1919), 234-254.
         [The extent to which French, English and Irish were used.]

Ir.5.   R. E. Davies, 'The Language Position in Eire', in the author's *Bilingualism in Wales*, Cape Town/Wynberg/Johannesburg, 1954, pp. 57-73.

Ir.5a.   A. Demangeon, 'La situation linguistique et l'état économique de l'Ouest irlandais', in *Annales de géographie*, 36 (1927), 169-173.

Ir.6.   T. O. Domhnallain, 'Bilingual Education in Ireland', in *Bulletin No. 6*, Faculty of Education, University College of Wales, Aberystwyth, 1959, 6-8.

Ir.7.   D. Simon Evans, 'Y Gwyddel a'i iaith: yr argyfwng', in *Y Traethodydd*, 115 (1960), 97-111.
         [In Welsh: 'The Irish and their language: the crisis'.]

Ir.7a.   E. Fels, 'Die Wiederbelebung der irischen Sprache', in *Petermanns Mitteilungen*, 73 (1927), 37-41.

Ir.8.   T. W. Freeman, *Ireland, a General and Regional Geography*, London, 3rd ed., 1965 (first published as *Ireland: its physical, historical, social and economic geography*, 1950).
         ['The Irish Language', pp. 165-170.]

Ir.9.   Tony Gray, *The Irish Answer*, London, 1966, 411 pp., Chapter X, 'Through the Medium (The Irish Language)', pp. 217-230.
         [A well-balanced overall survey.]

Ir.10. R. G. Gregg, 'Notes on the phonology of a County Antrim Scotch-Irish Dialect', in *Orbis*, VII (1958), 392-406.

[Deals with the English dialect of the area, but a map—p. 393—shows the Irish-speaking parts of Ulster a hundred years ago and today.]

Ir.11. H. Gaidoz, 'La Société pour la Conservation de la langue irlandaise', in *Revue Celtique*, IV (1879-80), 457-459.

[An account of the work of the Society for the Preservation of Irish, and some thoughts on the state of the language.]

Ir.11a. M. W. Heslinga, *The Irish Border as a Cultural Divide*, Assen, 1962, 225 pp.

[=University of Utrecht, *Sociaal Geografische Studies*, No. 6] [Comments *passim* on the situation of the Irish language; see Index, p. 221, under heading 'Gaelic Language in Ireland'.]

Ir.12. Nils M. Holmer, *The Dialects of Co. Clare*, Part I, Dublin, 1962, 186 pp.

[The introduction contains comments on the decline both in the use of Irish and in the quality of the Irish spoken.]

Ir.13. Nils M. Holmer, *The Irish Language in Rathlin Is., Co. Antrim*, Dublin, 1942, 247 pp.

[Contains comments on the decline both in the use of Irish and in the quality of the Irish spoken.]

Ir.14. Douglas Hyde, 'Irish as a Spoken Language', in the author's *Literary History of Ireland*, London, 1899, 608-637.

Ir.15. C. Kearns, 'The Revival of Irish', in *Irish Ecclesiastical Record*, 81 (1954), 184-195.

[Argues that Irish national survival depends on the survival of the Irish language.]

Ir.16. G. Lehmacher, 'Some thoughts on an Irish literary language', with comments by Most Rev. Dr. Sheehan, Prof. O. Bergin, Rev. F. W. O'Connell, Prof. T. F. O'Rahilly, Prof. T. Ó Máille, in *Studies*, XII (1923), 26-44.

[Lehmacher urges the need for the creation of a unified literary language. The discussion bears mainly on (a) the problems involved, and (b) the prior need to save the spoken language.]

Ir.17.   D. Myrddin Lloyd, 'The Irish Language Revival', in *The Welsh Anvil*, 4 (1952), 70-81.

Ir.18.   S. P. MacEnri, 'The Present Position and Prospects of the Irish Language', in *The Celtic Conference, 1917: Reports*, Perth, 1919, 32-54.

Ir.19.   John Macnamara, *Bilingualism and Primary Education: a Study of Irish Experience*, Edinburgh, 1966, x-173 pp.
[See specially pp. 3-6, an historical account of the movement to "restore" Irish through the schools; 131-133, dealing *inter alia* with the time devoted to Irish in schools; 135-138, Conclusion.]

Ir.20.   John Macnamara, *The Irish Language as a medium of instruction for children from English-speaking homes*, unpublished B.Ed. thesis, University of Edinburgh, 1959.

Ir.21.   John Macnamara, *The use of Irish in teaching children from Irish-speaking homes: a survey of Irish national schools*, unpublished Ph.D. thesis, University of Edinburgh, 1963.

Ir.22.   A. Marsh, 'The Revival of the Irish Language', in *The Year Book of Education*, 1949, 157-167.
[A historical survey of the situation of Irish before independence and observations, mainly critical, of the educational policy of the state.]

Ir.22a. J. Mescal, *Religion in the Irish System of Education*, Dublin, 1957, 253 pp.
[Chapter 2, 'The struggle for principles on which to found a system', pp. 32-76, contains numerous observations on the place of the Irish language in the Irish educational system.]

Ir. 23a Máire Cruise O'Brien, 'The Two Languages,' in *Conor Cruise O'Brien introduces Ireland*, ed. Owen Dudley Edwards, London, 1969, pp. 43-60.

Ir.23.   Gerard Murphy, 'Irish in our Schools, 1922-1945', in *Studies*, 37 (1948), 421-428.
[Critical of the methods adopted, which have achieved little.]

Ir.24. S. Ó Casaide, *The Irish Language in Belfast and Co. Down, A.D. 1601-1850*, Dublin, 1930, 69 pp.

[Revised and amplified version of an article first published in the *Down and Connor Historical Society's Journal*, II (1929), 4-63.]

Ir.25. B. Ó Cuív, *Irish Dialects and Irish-Speaking Districts*, Dublin, 1951, 95 pp. + 2 maps.

[Three lectures: I, The Gaeltacht—Past and present; II, Irish a living language; III, Some aspects of Cork dialects.]

Ir.25a B. Ó Cuív, 'Education and Language', in Desmond Williams (editor), *The Irish Struggle, 1916-1926*, London, 1966, pp. 153-166.

Ir.25b. B. Ó Cuív (editor), *A View of the Irish Language*, Dublin, 1969 156 pp.

[Consists of the twelve Thomas Davis lectures, broadcast in 1966, having as their general theme the Irish language. The following lectures are of particular relevance to the present bibliography:

(i) B. Ó Cuív, 'The changing form of the Irish language', pp. 22-34

(ii) M. Brennan, 'Language, personality and the nation', pp. 70-80

(iii) M. Wall, 'The Decline of the Irish Language', pp. 81-90

(iv) T. Ó hAilín, 'The Irish Revival Movements' pp. 91-100

(v) T. Ó Fiaich, 'The Language and Political History', pp. 101-111

(vi) C. Ó Danachair, 'The Gaeltacht', pp. 112-121

(vii) B. Ó Cuív, 'Irish in the Modern World', pp. 122-132. See also, pp. 138-140, three linguistic maps based on the reports of the 1851, 1891 and 1961 censuses.]

Ir.26. E. F. O'Doherty, 'Bilingual School Policy', in *Studies*, 47 (1958), 259-268.

[Argues that the present language policy of the state is not properly thought out and recommends that "attainable ideals should be clearly formulated and that realistic means capable of achieving these ideals should be adopted".]

Ir.27. John O'Flynn, *"Provincialisms" and "Dialects" in modern spoken Irish*, Dublin, 1910, 39 pp.
[Argues, not always very convincingly, that the differences between various regional forms of Irish, and the difficulties arising therefrom, have sometimes been exaggerated.]

Ir.28. T. F. O'Rahilly, *Irish Dialects Past and Present*, Dublin, 1932, 12 + 279 pp.
[Ch. XX, 'An Historical Retrospect', pp. 248-284, surveys the relationship between dialects and literary language.]

Ir.29. M. L. Sjoestedt, 'L'influence de la langue anglaise sur un parler local irlandais', in *Étrennes de linguistique offertes . . . à Émile Benveniste*, Paris, 1928, 81-122.
[The anglicizing influences at work on Irish pronunciation, vocabulary, idiom and syntax.]

Ir.30. M. L. Sjoestedt-Jonval, 'La littérature qui se fait en Irlande', in *Études Celtiques*, II (1937), 334-346.
[Bibliographical survey of contemporary publications of all kinds in Irish.]

Ir.31. J. E. Southall, 'Cornish and Irish', in the author's *Wales and her language*, Newport and London, 1892, pp. 365-375.
[The chapter referred to contains some useful facts on the activities of the Society for the Preservation of the Irish Language and on the teaching of Irish in schools.]

Ir.32. G. von Tevenar, 'Zur Sprachstatistik der irischen Volkszählungen von 1926 und 1936', in *Zeitschrift für celtische Philologie*, 22 (1941), 307-324.

Ir.33. G. Thomson, 'The Irish Language Revival', in *Yorkshire Celtic Studies*, III (=Yorkshire Society for Celtic Studies, *Transactions*, 1940-46), 3-12.
[A critical assessment of the Irish government's language policy and its comparative lack of success.]

Ir.34. M. Tierney, 'The Revival of the Irish Language,' followed by comments by General R. Mulcahy, Prof. P. Browne, Prof. O. Bergin and Prof. Liam O Briain, in *Studies*, XVI (1927), 1-22.
[A discussion of the problems involved in "reviving" Irish. This article is the subject of a note in *Revue Celtique*, 44 (1927), 475-476.]

Ir.34a.　H. Wagner, *Linguistic Atlas and Survey of Irish Dialects*, Vol. 1, *Introduction*, Dublin 1958.

[Pp. ix-xvii give details, based on a survey made between 1949 and 1956, of the extent to which Irish survived at that time in 88 different places in Ireland, and a map on which the extent to which Irish is spoken in various parts of the country is indicated by symbols.]

Ir.34b.　H. Wagner, 'A linguistic atlas and survey of Irish dialects', in *Lochlann*, I (1958), 9-48.

[Gives details of the extent to which Irish survives in various localities.]

Ir.35.　*The Census of Ireland for the Year 1861*, Part V, General Report, Dublin, 1864.

[Pp. xxxvi-xxxvii, figures for the Irish-speaking population, by provinces, counties, cities and towns.]

Ir.36.　*Census of Ireland, 1871*, Part I, Dublin, 1872-74. Vol. I, *Province of Leinster*, (1872); Vol. II, *Province of Munster* (1873); Vol. III, *Province of Ulster* (1874); Vol. IV, *Province of Connaught* (1874).

[In the report on each county, figures for Irish-speakers are given by baronies, in Table XXXVII.]

idem, Part III, *General Report*, Dublin, 1876.

[Tables LXXXIV and LXXXV, pp. 189-190, give figures for the Irish-speaking population by administrative areas and by age-groups respectively.]

Ir.37.　*Census of Ireland, 1881*, Part I, Dublin, 1881-82. Vol. I. *Province of Leinster* (1881); Vol. II, *Province of Munster* (1882); Vol. III, *Province of Ulster* (1882); Vol. IV, *Province of Connaught* (1882).

[In the report on each county, figures for Irish-speakers are given, by baronies, in Table XXXIV.]

idem, Part II, *General Report*, Dublin, 1882.

[Section XII, *Irish-speaking population* (pp. 73-74), contains general comment. Tables 157 (p. 375) and 158 (p. 376) give figures for Irish-speakers by administrative areas and by age-groups respectively.]

Ir.38.　*Census of Ireland, 1891*, Part I, Dublin, 1892.

[In the report on each county, figures for Irish-speakers are given, by baronies, in Table XXXIV.]

idem, Part II, *General Report*, Dublin, 1892.

[Section XI, *Irish-speaking population* (pp. 72-73) contains general comment. Tables 155 and 156 (pp. 525-526) give figures for Irish-speakers by administrative areas and by age-groups respectively.]

Ir.39.   *Census of Ireland, 1901*, Part I, Dublin, 1902.

[In the report on each county, figures for Irish-speakers are given, by County Districts, in Table XXXVII.]
idem, Part II, *General Report*, Dublin, 1902.

[Section XI, *Irish-speaking population* (pp. 72-73) contains general comment. Tables 165 (p. 575) and 166 (p. 576) give figures for Irish-speakers by administrative areas (which are not the same as those for which figures are given in previous reports) and by age-groups respectively.]

Ir.40.   *Census Returns for Ireland, 1911. Province of Leinster; Province of Munster; Province of Ulster; Province of Connaught;* each Dublin, 1912-13.

[In the report on each county, figures for Irish-speakers are given, by County Districts and District Electoral Divisions, in Table XXXVII.]
Census of Ireland, 1911, Part II, *General Report*, Dublin, 1913,

[Introduction, X, *Irish-speaking population* (pp. lvii-lix), general comment; Table 142, *Irish-speaking population* (p. 291), summary table.
A summary of the figures for this census is given, with comments, in *Revue Celtique*, 33 (1912), 483-486, with an additional note, *idem*, 34 (1913), 348.]

Ir.41.   Department of Industry and Commerce, *Census of Population of Ireland, 1926*, Vol. VIII, *Irish Language*, Dublin, 1932.

['La langue irlandaise en Irlande,' in *Revue Celtique*, 50 (1933), 197-199, is based on a newspaper report of the results of the 1926 census.]

Ir.42.   Department of Industry and Commerce, *Census of Population of Ireland, 1936*, Vol. VIII, *Irish Language*, Dublin, 1940.

[A note, 'La situation linguistique en Irlande', based on a newspaper report of the results of the 1936 census, is published in *Études Celtiques*, 4 (1948), 177-179.]

Ir.43.   Central Statistics Office, *Census of population of Ireland, 1946*, Vol. VIII, *Irish Language*, Dublin, 1953.
[This report is the subject of a note in *Études Celtiques*, 6 (1953-54), 203-206.]

Ir.44.   Central Statistics Office, *Census of Population of Ireland, 1961*, Vol. IX, *Irish Language*, Dublin, 1966.

Ir.45.   Coimisiún na Gaeltachta, *Report*, Dublin, 1926, 133 pp.
[The report of the special Commission set up in 1925 to study the situation of the Irish language. The report is accompanied by two maps, in a separate folder, showing the number and percentage of Irish-speakers in the Irish-speaking areas in 1911 and 1925 respectively. N.B. the Second Appendix (pp. 73-108) to the report, giving the figures for the *Special Census* (relating to the Irish-speaking population) of the *Gaeltacht* taken in August, 1925. There are also 25 leaflets, each with separate pagination, of minutes of evidence submitted to the Commission at various dates in 1925. The report is summarized by J. Vendryes, 'État de la langue irlandaise en Irlande', in *Revue Celtique*, 43 (1926), 461-464.]

Ir.45a.   Irish National Teachers' Organisation, *Report of Committee of Enquiry into the use of Irish as a teaching medium to children whose home language is English*, Dublin, 1941, 76 pp.

Ir.46.   Commission on the Restoration of the Irish Language, *Summary, in English, of the Final Report*, Dublin, 1963, 143 pp.
[Report of an official Commission, set up in 1958, with the following terms of reference: "Having regard to the position at present reached in the endeavour to secure the restoration of the Irish language, to consider and advise as to the steps that should now be taken by the community and the State to hasten towards that end."
The report deals with the present situation of Irish in all its aspects and makes 288 recommendations.
For reactions to this report, see R. A. Breatnach, 'Irish Revival Considered', in *Studies* 53 (1964), 18-30, J. Macnamara, 'The Commission on Irish: Psychological Aspects', *ibid.*, 164-173, M. Brennan, 'The restoration of Irish', *ibid.*, 263-277, J. Cunnane, 'Irish Language Commission's Report: reactions and reflections,' in *Irish Ecclesiastical Record*, 101 (1964), 145-153.
See also Nos. 47, 48 and 49 below.]

Ir.47.　*The Restoration of the Irish Language*, Dublin, 1965, 181 pp.

[Sets out the Irish Government's general policy on the Irish language, its views in the Report of the Commission on the Restoration of the Irish Language (see No. 46 above), and the action it proposes to take on the Commission's recommendations. See also Nos. 48 and 49 below.]

Ir.48.　*White Paper on the Restoration of the Irish Language. Progress report for the period ended 31 March, 1966*, Dublin, 1966, 39 pp.

[Records steps taken to implement the 1965 White Paper, No. 47 above. See also No. 49 below.]

Ir.49.　*White Paper on the Restoration of the Irish Language. Progress report for the period ended 31 March, 1968*, Dublin, 1969, 45 pp.

[Records further steps taken to implement the 1965 White Paper, No. 47 above.]

Ir.50.　Government of Ireland, *Gaeltacht Areas Order*, Dublin, 1956, 11 pp.

[The official list of Gaeltacht areas.]

Ir.51.　Government of Ireland, *Gaeltacht Areas Order*, Dublin, 1967, 5 pp.

[Additions to No. 50 above.]

XII. Manx

Man.1.　D. Campbell, 'The Isle of Man—its history and language', in *Transactions of the Gaelic Society of Inverness*, XII (1885-1886), 167-180.

[Some comments, p. 177, on the state of the language.]

Man.2.　F. J. Carmody, 'Spoken Manx', in *Zeitschrift für celtische Philologie*, 24 (1954), 58-80.

[Some account, pp. 59-60, of the last native speakers of Manx.]

Man.3. A. S. B. Davies, 'Cyflwr presennol Iaith Geltaidd Ynys Manaw' (='The Present state of the Celtic Language of the Isle of Man'), in *Bulletin of the Board of Celtic Studies*, XII, 4 (May, 1948), 89-91.

[Although written in Welsh, this article is included here as it lists, p. 90, the twenty remaining native speakers of Manx the author was able to trace on the island in August, 1946.]

Man.4. K. H. Jackson, *Contributions to the Study of Manx Phonology*, Edinburgh, 1955, x-149 pp.

[Pp. 1-4 include some remarks on the state of the language and list ten speakers still alive in December, 1950.]

Man.5. H. Jenner, 'The Manx Language: its grammar, literature and present state', in *Transactions of the Philological Society*, 1875-1876, 172-197.

[Valuable especially for its analysis of Jenner's unofficial census of Manx speakers carried out in 1874.]

Man.6. J. J. Kneen, *A Grammar of the Manx Language*, London, 1931, xii-209 pp.

[The Historical Introduction, pp. 1-30, is important for the purposes of the present bibliography; *inter alia*, it lists, pp.10-14, all known publications in Manx.]

Man.7. W. S. Lach-Szyrma, 'Manx and Cornish: The Dying and the Dead', in *Journal of the British Archaeological Association*, 44 (1888), 273-278.

[Some comments, based on personal observation, on the decline of Manx.]

Man.8. A. Moore, 'An historical sketch of the Manx Language, with some account of its literature', in *Transactions of the Celtic Society of Montreal*, 1887, 70-83.

[Reproduces various contemporary references, 16th-19th centuries, to the state of the language.]

Man.9. A. W. Moore, 'An historical sketch of the Manx language with an account of the sources from which a knowledge of it can be acquired', in *Yn Lioar Manninagh* (Journal of the Isle of Man Natural History and Antiquarian Society), I (1889-1892), 129-134.

[Lists the only eight remaining monoglot Manx-speakers to be found in 1884.]

Man.10. *Census 1901. Islands in the British Seas*, London, 1903.

[*Isle of Man*, Table 18, gives the figures for Manx speakers, a total of 4,657, including fifty-nine speaking Manx only. It must be pointed out that the figures for Manx in census reports become increasingly unreliable from one census to another. See in particular our comment on the 1961 census, No. 15 below.]

Man.11. *Census 1911. Islands in the British Seas*, London, 1913.

[Though figures for Manx-speakers were collected at the 1911 census, they are not given in the report. They are, however, to be found in 'The census of Manx speakers' in *Mannin*, No. 2, Nov. 1913, p. 80, where it is stated that the figure of thirty-one monoglot Manx-speakers is an obvious error.]

Man.12. *Census 1921, Isle of Man*, London, 1924.

[Figures for Manx-speakers—896 in all—are given in Table 16 and commented on on p. xv.]

Man.13. *Census, 1931. Isle of Man*, London, 1933.

[Figures for Manx-speakers—529 in all—are given in Table XVI and commented on on p.xxi.]

Man.14. *Census 1951. Report on the Isle of Man*, London, 1956.

[Figures for Manx-speakers—355 in all—are given in Table 26 and commented on on pp.xlvi-xlvii.]

Man.15. *Census 1961. Report on Isle of Man. Part II, Migration, Economic Activity and other topics*, London, 1966.

[Figures for Manx-speakers are given in Table 22. The unreliability of the census figures for Manx is revealed by the fact that, although only two native speakers were known to be alive in 1961, and although probably not more than two or three dozen other people had acquired a good working knowledge of the language, this report gives the number of Manx-speakers as 165.]

Man.16. 'Le celtique dans l'Ile de Man', in *Revue Celtique*, 44 (1927) 466-468; 46 (1929), 356-357.

[Various personal testimonies and census figures relating to the state of the language from the late 19th century onwards. See also *Revue celtique*, 47 (1930), 248.]

XIII. Occitan

Oc.1. P.-L. Berthaud, *Réflexions sur l'enseignement de la langue d'oc*, Vichy, 1942, 8 pp. (reprinted from the *Revue universelle*, 25.11.1941).

Oc.2. - Blanc, *Essai sur la substitution du français au provençal à Narbonne*, Paris, 1898, 40 pp. (reprinted from the *Bulletin historique et philologique*).

Oc.3. A. Brun, *L'introduction de la langue française en Béarn et en Roussillon*, Paris, 1923, 94 pp.

Oc.4. A. Brun, *La langue française en Provence, de Louis XIV au Félibrige*, Marseille, 1927, 169 pp.
[Abundant information on the situation of Provençal during the period in question.]

Oc.5. A. Brun, *Recherches historiques sur l'introduction du français dans les provinces du Midi*, Paris, 1923, xv-505 pp.

Oc.6. C. Costes, 'L'occitan dans les rues de Toulouse en 1956', in *Via Domitia*, IV (1957), 27-81.

Oc.7. T. Elwert, 'Della vitalità del provenzale e del felibrismo', in *Istituto lombardo di scienze e lettere, Rendiconti, Classe di lettere*, 85 (1952), 3-32.

Oc.8. R. Lafont, 'Remarques sur les conditions et les méthodes d'une étude rationnelle du comportement linguistique des Occitans', in *Annales de l'Institut d'Études Occitanes*, XI (15 mai 1952), 41-45.

Oc.9. P. Lagarde, 'Essai de statistique sur l'enseignement occitan,' in *Cahiers pédagogiques de l'Institut d'Études Occitanes*, No. 4 (ler trimestre, 1957-58), 2-4.
[List of secondary schools and universities in which Occitan is taught.]

Oc.10. J. Lesaffre, 'L'édition occitane de 1945 à 1965: essai de statistique bibliographique', in *Mélanges dédiés à la mémoire de Jean Boutière*, (forthcoming).
[An analysis of Occitan publications according to genre, dialect and orthographical system ("graphie félibréenne" or "graphie occitane").]

Oc.11.   B. Müller, 'Das Provenzalische in neuerer Zeit', in *Die neueren Sprachen*, XIII (1964), 413-429.

Oc.12.   P. Pansier, *Histoire de la langue provençale à Avignon du XIIe au XIXe siècle*, Vol. 4, *Évolution du provençal moderne*, Avignon, 1927, xiv-169 pp.

[See in particular Ch. II, pp. 16-25, 'Évolution linguistique', dealing especially with French infiltration into local speech; Ch. III, pp. 26-37, 'Morcellement de la langue provençale [=occitane]'; Chs. V-XIV, pp. 38-135, which are devoted to aspects of the organization and activity of the Félibrige, of which the author is sharply critical; Ch. XV, pp. 136-148, 'La question de l'enseignement du provençal', in which attention is drawn to the difficulties involved. (Vols. 1 and 2 of the work are devoted to the publication of various Provençal documents, 12th-16th centuries, and Vol. 3 to a glossary of the documents.)]

Oc.13.   Sully-André Peyre, *La Branche des Oiseaux*, Aigues-Vives, 1948, 190 pp.

[A highly polemical work in which it is urged that the Provençal dialect as codified and used by Mistral, should be considered, *par droit de chef d'œuvre*, as the only modern literary form of Occitan.]

Oc.14.   G. Price, 'The Problem of Modern Literary Occitan', in *Archivum Linguisticum*, XVI (1964), 34-53.

Oc.15.   E. Ripert, *Le provençal au baccalauréat. Enquête et conclusions*, Aix-en-Provence, 1925, 126 pp.

[The title given here is the one that figures on the title-page of the book. The cover bears the title *Doit-on admettre la langue de Mistral au baccalauréat*? The volume contains the replies given by thirty-seven writers, university teachers and politicians to a questionnaire sent out by Ripert, Ripert's conclusions, press comment, etc.]

Oc.16.   J. Roumanille, 'Dissertation sur l'orthographe provençale', pre-fixed (pp. v-lxviii) to his *La Part dau Bon Diéu*, Avignon, 1853, lxviii-243 pp.

Oc.17. J. Salvat, 'Contribution historique à la langue de Mistral', in *Actes et Mémoires du Premier Congrès International de Langue et Littérature du Midi de la France*, Avignon, 1957, 325-349.

[An account of the debating that went on around 1852-54 as to the extent to which the orthographical norms of the Félibres should take account of etymology.]

Oc.18. Ch. de Tourtoulon et O. Bringuier, *Étude sur la limite géographique de la langue d'oc et de la langue d'oïl*, Paris, 1876, 63 pp.

[Reprinted from *Archives des Missions scientifiques et littéraires*, 3e série, t. III, 545-605.
Contains a map, scale 1/320000, showing the limit from the Gironde to the department of the Creuse.]

Oc.19. J. Véran, 'La presse de langue d'oc', in *Mélanges Chabaneau*, Erlangen, 1907, pp. 1019-1024.

Oc.20. *Actualité de la langue provençale*, Saint-Rémy-de-Provence, 1955, 38 pp. (=Cahiers de culture provençale, publiés par le Groupement d'Études Provençales, No. 3).

[See especially pp. 4-9, C. Rostaing, 'Les conditions actuelles de la langue provençale'; pp. 15-20, C. Dourguin, 'Les moyens de maintenir la langue par l'école'; pp. 30-33, C. Mauron, 'Le droit de chef d'œuvre.']

Oc.21. *Défense des langues régionales de France et en particulier du provençal*, par quelques Toulonnais, Toulon, 1960, 8 pp.

Oc.22. 'La langue d'oc à l'école: Documents', in *Lo Gai Saber*, No. 243, Jan.-Feb., 1952, 414-416.

[Ministerial circulars relating to the implementation of the law of Jan. 1951, allowing a limited amount of time to be devoted to the teaching of regional languages.]

Oc.23. *Pour une pédagogie occitaniste*, Toulouse (Documents de l'Institut d'Études Occitanes), 1952, 31 pp.

Oc.24. *La réforme linguistique occitane et l'enseignement de la langue d'oc*, Toulouse (Documents de l'Institut d'Études Occitanes), 1950, 12 pp.

Oc.25. The *Bulletin trimestriel* of the association *Lou Prouvençau a l'Escolo* (Saint-Rémy-de-Provence) frequently publishes articles and documents relating to the teaching of Provençal—or of the regional languages of France in general—at various levels and to moves designed to improve the legal situation of these languages in state schools.

XIV. Romansh

R.1. Joh. Alton, *Die ladinischen Idiome in Ladinien, Gröden, Fassa, Buchenstein, Ampezzo*, Innsbruck, 1879, 379 pp.

R.2. E. L. Bähler, 'Die Pflege der Landessprachen an den schweizerischen Schulen', in *Archiv für das schweizerische Unterrichtswesen*, 31 (1945), 40-45.

R.3. C. Battisti, 'Il friulano letterario e le sue premesse', in *VIII Congresso internazionale di Studi romanzi (Firenze*, 1956), Atti, II, Florence, 1960, 59-71.

R.4. C. Battisti, *Popoli e lingue nell'Alto Adige*, Florence, 1931, xi-401 pp.
[See Ch. X, 'Le condizioni linguistiche attuali nell'Alto Adige', and in particular section 2 thereof (pp. 370-375) which deals with the extent to which Ladin is spoken in the area. N.B. Battisti is one of those who deny the fundamental linguistic unity of the Romansh dialects of Graubünden, the Ladin dialects of the Dolomitic valleys and Friulan.]

R.5. C. Battisti, *Storia della "questione ladina"*, Florence, 1937, vii-85 pp.
[Mainly devoted to a criticism of the "unitary" view of Romansh.]

R.6. C. Battisti, *Storia linguistica e nazionale delle valli dolomitiche atesine*, Florence, 1941, 331 pp.

R.7. A. Baur, *Wo steht das Rätoromanische heute?* (Sonderdruck aus dem Jahrbuch der eidgenössischen Räte, 1955), n.p. (Lia Rumantscha), 1955, 82 pp.
[An overall survey of the position of Romansh in the Grisons.]

R.8.   F. Berther, 'Der Rückgang der romanischen Sprache in Graubünden', in *Monatsschrift für christliche Sozialreform*, 31. Jahrgang, Sept., 1909.

R.9.   R. R. Bezzola, 'La formazione di una lingua scritta ladina nei Grigioni', in *Ce Fastu*? 31 (1955), 15-26.

R.10.   R. R. Bezzola, *Wesen und Problematik der vierten Landessprache* (Schriften des Schweizerischen Lehrervereins, No. 33), Zürich, 1958, 27 pp.

R.11.   G. Caduff, *Die sprachliche Situation von Romanisch-Bünden*, Chur, 1947, 16 pp.

R.12.   P. Cavigelli, *Die Germanisierung von Bonaduz* (in preparation). [This reference is taken from A. Widmer, 'Der Stand der Bündner-romanischen Linguistik', in *Communications et Rapports du Premier Congrès international de Dialectologie générale* (1960), Louvain, 1965, 283-301 (p. 295); the work is now said to be completed—see A. Widmer, 'Der Stand der bündnerromanischen Linguistik,' in *Orbis*, XV (1966), 560-574 (p. 573).]

R.13.   A. Decurtins, *La Suisse rhétoromane et la défense de sa latinité*, Fribourg, 1959, 32 pp.

R.14.   G. Deplazes, 'Geschichte der sprachlichen Schulbücher im romanischen Rheingebiet,' in *Arbeiten zur Psychologie, Pädagogik und Heilpädagogik*, I (1949), x-203 pp.

R.15.   Paul Fink, *Niedergang und Wiederaufstieg des Rätoromanischen*, Zürich, 1946, 40 pp.

R.16.   G. Francescato, 'Il friulano, oggi', in *Orbis*, VII (1958), 198-204.

R.17.   G. Francescato, 'Saggio statistico sul friulano a Udine,' in *Ce Fastu*? 32 (1956).

R.18.   Th. Gartner, *Raetoromanische Grammatik*, Heilbronn, 1883, xlviii-208 pp. [See especially pp. xix-xxxviii, *Name, Grenzen und Theile*.]

R.19.   Th. Gartner, *Handbuch der rätoromanischen Sprache und Literatur*, Halle, 1910, lxviii-391 pp.
[See especially pp. 1-8 on the geographical extent of the different dialects and pp. 273-386, 'Rätoromanisches Schrifttum', containing *inter alia* an account of the use made of the various dialects for literary purposes. The different dialects are defined and their status as literary languages briefly commented on in Gartner's contribution, *Die rätoromanischen Mundarten*, to Gröber's *Grundriss der romanischen Philologie*, I, Strassburg, 1888, 461-488, especially pp. 461-463.]

R.20.   Gian-Reto Gieré, *Die Rechtsstellung des rätoromanischen in der Schweiz*, Winterthur, 1956, xv-125 pp.

R.21.   C. Hegnauer, *Das Sprachenrecht der Schweiz*, Zürich, 1947, xvi-319 pp.

R.22.   Luigi Heilmann, 'Problemi della ladinia dolomitica', in *Ce Fastu?* 38 (1962), 5-10.

R.23.   A. Kuhn, 'Das Ladinische im 16. Jahrhundert rund um Silvretta und Rätikon', in *Festschrift Karl Pivec*, Innsbruck 1966 (=Innsbrucker Beiträge zur Kulturwissenschaft, Bd. 12), 247-255.
[Evidence from Chiampel, *Raetiae alpestris topographica descriptio* (*c.* 1570/71), for Romansh in a now entirely German-speaking area on the Swiss-Austrian border.]

R.24.   Peider Lansel, *I Retoromanci*, Milan, 1935.
[Translations: *Die Rätoromanen*, Frauenfeld, 1936; *Les Rhéto-romans*, Neuchâtel, 1936; *Ils Retorumantschs*, Samaden, 1936; *The Raeto-Romans*, Chur, 1937.]

R.25.   W. A. Liebeskind, *Die romanische Schweiz als nationales Problem*, 2nd ed., Glarus, 1936, 14 pp.

R.26.   H. Lüdtke, 'Inchiesta sul confine dialettale tra il veneto e il friulano,' in *Orbis*, VI (1957), 122-125.

R.27.   K. D. McRae, *Switzerland: Example of Cultural Coexistence* (Canadian Institute of International Affairs, Contemporary Affairs No. 33), Toronto, 1964, 74 pp.
[Remarks on Romansh *passim*, drawing attention particularly to its inferior prestige as compared with the three official languages.]

R.28.   K. Mayer, 'Cultural Plurism and Linguistic Equilibrium in Switzerland', in *American Sociological Review*, 16 (1951), 156-163.

[Comments and figures relating to the distribution of the four national languages during the preceding century. Of little interest.]

R.29.   H. Morf, 'Ein Sprachenstreit in der rätischen Schweiz', in *Aus Dichtung und Sprache der Romanen*, I, Strasbourg, 1903, 418-463.

[Originally published as an article in 1888 under the title 'Die sprachliche Einheitsbestrebung in der rätischen Schweiz'. Devoted mainly to a penetrating and damaging criticism of Bühler's misconceived and unsuccessful attempt in the late 19th century to create a highly artificial common literary language for all the dialects. Also contains interesting comments on the state of the language, and views—generally pessimistic—on its future prospects.]

R.30.   G. B. Pellegrini, 'Osservazioni sul confine del ladino centrale', in *Studi mediolatini e volgari*, I (1953), 127-154.

R.31.   C. Pult, *Rätoromanisch, unsere vierte Landessprache*, St. Gallen, 1938, 27 pp.

R.32.   J. Pult, 'Der rätoromanische Sonderfall', in *Schweizerisches Nationales Jahrbuch: Die Schweiz*, 1951, pp. 166-170.

R.33.   A. Sartorius, 'Die fortschreitende Verdeutschung der Rätoromanen in Graubünden', in *Deutsche Erde*, IV (1905), 56-59.

R.34.   A. Sartorius, Freiherr von Waltershausen, 'Die Germanisierung der Rätoromanen in der Schweiz: volkswirtschaftliche und national-politische Studien', in *Forschungen zur deutschen Landes- und Volkskunde*, XII (1899-1900), 365-474.

[Contains chapters on the *statistische Grundlage*, the linguistic border, the recession of Romansh, the position of Romansh in schools and churches, etc.]

R.35.   E. Thilo, *Note sur l'égalité et sur l'usage des langues nationales en Suisse*, Lausanne, 1941.

R.36.　　Giorgio del Vecchio, *Le valli della morente italianità: il "ladino"*
al bivio, nuova ed. con appendici, Florence, 1960, 45 pp.

[The title chapter was originally published as an article in *Nuova*
Antologia in 1912.

Devoted mainly, but not exclusively, to the Romansh of the
Grisons; contains various observations on the state of the
language.]

R.37.　　A. Widmer, 'Das Rätoromanische in Graubünden', in *Orbis*, XIV
(1965), 560-571.

[Useful survey, falling into three sections: 1, Die Geschichte des
Bündnerromanischen; 2, Die Renaissance des Bündnerromanischen; 3, Die jetztige Lage des Bündnerromanischen.]

R.38.　　P. Wunderli, 'Zur Regression des Bündnerromanischen' in *Vox*
Romanica, 25 (1966), 56-81.

[An analysis, on the basis of the census reports for 1888, 1920
and 1960, of the decline of Romansh in Graubünden.]

R.39.　　*Eidgenössische Volkszählung*, 1. *Dez*. 1960, Band II, *Graubünden*,
Eidgenössisches statistisches Amt, Bern, 1964, Statistische Quel-
lenwerke der Schweiz, Heft 374.

[Contains the figures for Romansh-speakers in Graubünden
obtained at the most recent census.]

XV. Sardinian

Culturally, Sardinian is a highly underprivileged language even when
compared with any of the other languages covered by this bibliography.
Consequently, though there are numerous studies relating to the structure
and vocabulary of Sardinian (see in particular M. T. Atzori, *Bibliografia*
di linguistica sarda, 1953; id., *Bibliografia di linguistica sarda, 1952-1956*,
1959; *Bibliografia di linguistica sarda, 1948-1959*, 1962), there is
little of relevance to this bibliography. The works listed here relate only
marginally to the present position of the language.

Sard.1.　　M. F. M. Meiklejohn, 'Profilittu 'e limba sarda,' in *Italian Studies*
presented to E. R. Vincent, 1962, 294-311.

["The purpose of this paper is to give a short account of the
Sardinian language in English, something which has never been
reliably attempted before."]

Sard.2.   A. Sanna, *Introduzione agli studi di linguistica sarda*, Cagliari, 1957, 227 pp.
[The following chapters give an account of the use of various dialects for literary purposes at different periods: *I primi studi*, pp. 23-31; *Testi moderni*, pp. 67-79; *La divisione dialettale*, pp. 207-215.]

Sard.3.   M. L. Wagner, *La lingua sarda. Storia, spirito e forma*, Bern, 1951, 419 pp.
[See especially Ch. XVI, *I dialetti sardi*, 387-404; Ch. XVII, *La lingua della poesia*, 405-416.]

XVI. Scots

Sc.1.   Marjorie Bald, 'The Pioneers of Anglicised Speech in Scotland', in *Scottish Historical Review*, 24 (1927), 179-193.
[The influence of English on Scots and the use of English by Scottish writers in the 16th and 17th centuries.]

Sc.2.   J. C. Catford, 'The Linguistic Survey of Scotland', in *Orbis*, VI (1957), 105-121.
[Though concerned mainly with the methodology of a dialectal survey, this article contains numerous remarks on the history, distribution and present position of Scots (which is here taken to be a variety of English).]

Sc.3.   James Colville, *Studies in Lowland Scots*, Edinburgh and London, 1909, ix-331 pp.
[Much of this curious book has nothing to do with Scots (e.g. Section I, 'The Dawn', which is largely devoted to Gothic). The following sections however contain a certain amount of relevant information on the history and contemporary state of Scots: II, 'In Decadence' (pp. 59-108); III, 'Field Philology', (pp.109-164).]

Sc.4.   D. Craig, *Scottish Literature and the Scottish People, 1680-1830*, London, 1961, 340 pp.
[See especially Ch. VIII, pp. 235-269, 'Literature and Native Language', which discusses and evaluates the use of English and different shades of Scots by Scottish writers and questions the desirability of "establishing synthetic Scots" as a literary medium.]

Sc.5.   Sir W. A. Craigie, 'The Present State of the Scottish Tongue', in Sir W. A. Craigie and others, *The Scottish Tongue*, London, 1924, pp. 3-46.

Sc.6.   Sir W. A. Craigie and A. J. Aitken, 'Scottish Language', in *Chambers's Encyclopaedia*, 1967 edition, XII, 339-340.

Sc.7.   William Grant (editor), *The Scottish National Dictionary*, Vol. I, Edinburgh, n.d., *Introduction*, I, viii-xli.
[Contains *inter alia* a study—with a map—of the geographical limits of Scots, a historical survey, and incidental comments on the present position of the language.]

Sc.8.   W. Grant, Introduction (pp. ix-xxiii) to A. Warrack, *A Scots Dialect Dictionary*, London and Edinburgh, 1911, xxiv-717 pp.
[Grant's introduction traces the external history of Scots, the causes of its decadence, dialectal divisions, etc.]

Sc.9.   A. Gray, 'Lallans: a plea for the Kail-yard', in *Burns Chronicle & Club Directory*, Second Series, Vol. 25 (1950), 9-13.
[Literature that is meant to be *read* is outside the scope of Scots, but it is a suitable vehicle for literature that is meant to be *heard*.]

Sc.10.   C. M. Grieve, 'The New Movement in Vernacular Poetry,' in the author's *Contemporary Scots Studies*, London, 1926, Ch.23.
[Some general reflections and a particular study of two poets.]

Sc.11.   J. Kinsley, 'The Decay of Lowland Scots', in *The Welsh Anvil*, 4 (1952), 61-63.

Sc.12.   H. Kloss, *Die Entwicklung neuer germanischer Kultursprachen von 1800 bis 1950*, Munich, 1952, pp. 112-119.

Sc.13.   Hugh MacDiarmid, 'The Case for Synthetic Scots,' in the author's *At the Sign of the Thistle*, London, n.d. [1934?], 177-196.

Sc.14.   Lillian E. C. MacQueen, *The Last Stages of the Older Literary Language of Scotland: a study of the surviving Scottish elements in Scottish prose, 1700-1750*, unpublished Ph.D. thesis, University of Edinburgh, 1957.

Sc.15.   Sir J. A. H. Murray, 'The Dialects of the Southern Counties of Scotland', in *Transactions of the Philological Society*, 1872, 251 pp. + map.

[Contains a historical and geographical survey, and an account of the literary use of the language.]

Sc.16.   G. Gregory Smith, *Scottish Literature: Character and Influence*, London, 1919, viii-296 pp.

[See Ch. V, pp. 130-154, 'The Problem of Dialect', especially pp. 137-154.]

Sc.17.   J. C. Smith, 'Scots and English', in *University of Edinburgh Journal*, Autumn 1934, 16-25.

[Deals, *inter alia*, with the linguistic position of Scots (it is argued that it *is* a distinct language from English), and presents some thoughts on the present position and prospects of Scots.]

Sc.18.   G. Wagner, 'The Use of Lallans for Prose', in *Journal of English and Germanic Philology*, 51 (1952), 212-225.

Sc.19.   Sir James Wilson, *The Dialects of Central Scotland*, London, 1926, 276 pp.

[See pp. 168-225, 'The Spelling of Scotch', a historical survey, from the 16th century to the present day, with recommendations for the future spelling of Scots.]

Sc.20.   Douglas Young, *"Plastic Scots" and the Scottish Literary Tradition*, n.p., 1946, 32 pp.

[An answer, based on historical and linguistic arguments, to the charge that contemporary literary Scots is "plastic Scots", i.e. an artificial language.]

Sc.21.   Douglas Young, *The Use of Scots for Prose*, Greenock (Papers of Greenock Philosophical Society), 1949, 20 pp. (John Galt lecture for 1949).

[A historical survey with some observations on the present situation.]

Sc.22.   Douglas Young, 'Whither the "Scottish Renaissance"?' in *Forum for Modern Language Studies*, II (1966), 386-395.

[Observations on the history of literary Scots, the competition from English, and the use of Scots for poetry in recent years.]

XVII. Scottish Gaelic

SG.1.   W. Bannerman, *On the Extinction of Gaelic in Buchan and Lower Banffshire*, Banff, 1895, 29 pp.
[Reprinted from the *Banffshire Journal*, Oct.-Nov., 1895.]

SG.2.   J. L. Campbell, *Gaelic in Scottish Education and Life: Past, Present and Future*, 2nd ed., revised and extended, Edinburgh, 1950, 122 pp. (first ed., 1945).

SG.3.   J. L. Campbell, 'Scottish Gaelic in Canada' in *American Speech*, April, 1936, 128-136.
[This article is summarized in *Études Celtiques*, II (1937), 214-215. An earlier article by the same author, 'Scottish Gaelic in Canada, An unofficial census', published in the newspaper *The Scotsman*, 31-I-1933, is the subject of a note in *Revue Celtique*, 50 (1933), 199-200.
See also Nos. 9, 10a, 17 and 28 below.]

SG.4.   C. W. Dunn, 'The Cultural Status of Scottish Gaelic: a Humanistic Interpretation', in *Modern Language Quarterly*, XXII (1961), 3-11.

SG.5.   John Hunter, 'Gaelic in the Presbytery of Dunkeld', in the author's *Diocese and Presbytery of Dunkeld*, 2 vols., London, 1918, II, 101-109.
[Various 17th, 18th and 19th century testimonies to the state of the language in the area.]

SG.6.   K. Jackson, 'The Situation of the Scottish Gaelic Language and the Work of the Linguistic Survey of Scotland', in *Lochlann* (Oslo), I (1958), 228-234.

SG.7.   W. L. Lorimer, 'The Persistence of Gaelic in Galloway and Carrick', in *Scottish Gaelic Studies*, VI (1949), 114-136, VII (1953), 26-46.
[Evidence for the persistence of Gaelic and the penetration of Scots in south-west Scotland in the 16th and 17th centuries.]

SG.7a. K. D. MacDonald, 'The Gaelic Language, its Study and Development', in *The Future of the Highlands* (ed. D. S. Thomson and I. Grimble), London, 1968, pp. 175-201.

SG.8.   G. W. Mackay, 'The Gaelic Question in Scotland,' in *The Celtic Conference, 1917: Reports*, Perth, 1919, 59-76.

[Gaelic in education, the churches, the press, etc.]

SG.9.   C. I. N. MacLeod, 'The Gaelic Tradition in Nova Scotia', in *Lochlann*, I (1958), 235-240.

[Further information on Gaelic in Canada is provided by the following:

(i) D. Aspey, 'Where the Gaelic lives: some notes on Cape Breton Scots', in *The Scots Magazine*, XIII (April - September, 1930), 425-429.

(ii) C. W. Dunn, 'Gaelic in Cape Breton', in *An Gaidheal*, XLIII (1947-48), 143-145 and 6b-9b, a report, based on personal investigation, of Gaelic in Cape Breton in 1941;

(iii) K. Jackson, 'Notes on the Gaelic of Port Hood, Nova Scotia', in *Scottish Gaelic Studies*, VI (1949), 89-109—this is devoted mainly to phonology, morphology and a selection of texts, but p. 89 has some comments on the decline of Gaelic in the town;

(iv) D. M. Sinclair, 'Gaelic Newspapers and Prose Writings in Nova Scotia', in *An Gaidheal*, 55 (1950), 35-36 and 40—a historical survey.

See also No. 3 above and Nos. 10a, 17 and 28 below.]

SG.10.   M. MacLeod, 'Gaelic in Highland Education', in *Transactions of the Gaelic Society of Inverness*, 43 (1960-63), 305-334.

[Historical survey.]

SG.10a. N. Matheson, 'Twilight over Gaeldom', in *Chambers's Journal*, Oct. 1952, 593 -597.

[On the decline of Gaelic in Scotland and Cape Breton Island.]

SG.11.   J. R. Morrison, 'Scottish Gaelic,' in *The Welsh Anvil*, IV (1952), 56-61.

[On the decline of Gaelic.]

SG.12.   J. A. H. Murray, 'Present Limits of the Celtic in Scotland', in *Transactions of the Philological Society*, 1870-72 [1875], Part II, 231-237, with a map; reprinted, with an introduction by Gaidoz and the map, in *Revue Celtique*, II (1873-75), 178-187.

SG.13. J. Nisbet, 'Bilingualism and the school,' in *Scottish Gaelic Studies*,
X (1963), 44-52.

[Reflections on the state of affairs revealed by the report on
Gaelic-speaking Children in Highland Schools, see below No. 29.]

SG.13a. A. C. O'Dell and Kenneth Walton, *The Highlands and Islands of
Scotland*, London & Edinburgh, 1962, xii-353 pp.

[See p. 147, 'Decline of Gaelic Speaking in Scotland,' consisting
of (a) a map showing numbers of Gaelic-speakers in Scotland in
1891 and (b) graphs showing the decline in percentage of Gaelic-
speakers in the various highland counties between 1881 and
1951.]

SG.14. G. Price, 'The decline of Scottish Gaelic in the Twentieth
Century', in *Orbis*, XV (1966), 365-387.

SG.15. J. Ross, 'Bilingualism and folk life', in *Scottish Studies*, VI (1962),
60-70.

[Contains comments on some anglicizing influences in north-west
Skye.]

SG.16. S. W. Semple, *The Problem of Bilingualism in the Schools of
Wales and Scotland*, Toronto, 1964, vii-47 pp. (University of
Toronto, Ontario College of Education, Educational Research
Series, No. 35).

[Scotland, Part II, pp. 25-47. Contains useful chapters on the
historical background and on various aspects of the present
situation of Welsh and Gaelic, and a bibliography that serves to
bring up to date that given in *Bilingualism* (see above II, *Bibliographies, Welsh*).]

SG.16a. J. A. Smith, 'The Position of Gaelic and Gaelic Culture in
Scottish Education', in *The Future of the Highlands* (ed.
D. S. Thomson and I. Grimble), London, 1968, pp. 57-91.

SG.17. J. Vendryes and J. L. Campbell, 'Le gaélique d'Écosse au Canada'
in *Revue Celtique*, 50 (1933), 199-200; 51 (1934), 161-162; *Études
Celtiques*, I (1936), 395-396.

SG.18. W. J. Watson, 'The History of Gaelic in Scotland', in *Transactions
of the Gaelic Society of Inverness*, 37 (1934-36), 115-135.

SG.19.   W. J. Watson, 'The Position of Gaelic in Scotland', in *Celtic Review*, X (1914-16), 69-84.

SG.20.   An Comunn Gaidhealach, *Report of Special Committee on the Teaching of Gaelic in Schools and Colleges*, Glasgow, 1936, 40 pp.

SG.21.   *Tenth Decennial Census of the Population of Scotland, taken 5th April, 1891*. Report, Vol. I, Edinburgh, 1892.
[P. xi, general comment on the Gaelic-speaking population. The tables for each county, in Parts I-V, give the figures for Gaelic-speakers in each administrative area and ecclesiastical parish.]

SG.22.   *Eleventh Decennial Census of the Population of Scotland, 1901*. Report, Vol. I, Glasgow, 1902.
[Note on Gaelic-speaking population, pp. xvi-xvii; the figures for Gaelic-speakers are given in Appendix Table XV, p. xxviii.]

SG.23.   *Census of Scotland, 1911. Report on the Twelfth Decennial Census of Scotland*, Vol. I, London, 1912-1913.
[The figures for Gaelic-speakers and a commentary are given in the introduction to the report on each county.]

SG.24.   *Census of Scotland, 1921. Report on the Thirteenth Decennial Census of Scotland*, Vol. I, Edinburgh, 1922-23.
[The figures for Gaelic-speakers are given in Table 26 of the report on each county, with a commentary in the introduction. The figures for Gaelic-speakers are summarized by J. Vendryes, 'État de la langue gaélique en Écosse,' in *Revue Celtique*, 44 (1927), 213-216.]

SG.25.   *Census of Scotland, 1931. Report on the Fourteenth Decennial Census of Scotland*, Vol. I, Edinburgh, 1932-33.
[The figures for Gaelic-speakers are given in Table 25 of the report on each county, with a commentary in the introduction.]

SG.26.   General Register Office, Edinburgh, *Census, 1951. Report on the Fifteenth Census of Scotland*, Vol. I, Edinburgh, 1953-54.
[The figures for Gaelic-speakers are given in Table 17 of the report on each county, with a commentary in the introduction.]

SG.27. General Register Office, Edinburgh, *Census, 1961, Scotland,* Vol. VII, *Gaelic,* 1966, xxiii-28 pp.

[For the first time, all figures relating to Gaelic-speakers are gathered together in a separate volume. The report is usefully supplemented by:
   General Register Office, Edinburgh, *Census 1961, Scotland,* Gaelic, Supplementary Leaflet (Leaflet No. 27), 1966, 8 pp., which reprints the table giving figures for Gaelic-speakers in each administrative division of Scotland (Table 1 of the report), with the addition of a column showing the percentage of Gaelic-speakers in each area.]

SG.28. The latest figures for Gaelic-speakers in Nova Scotia are given in: Dominion Bureau of Statistics/Bureau Fédéral de la Statistique, *1961 Census of Canada/Recensement du Canada, Vol: 1— Part:2, Population, Official Language and Mother Tongue/Langue officielle et langue maternelle,* Ottawa, 1963.

SG.29. *Gaelic-Speaking Children in Highland Schools* (Publications of the Scottish Council for Research in Education, No. xlvii), London, 1961, 91 pp.

[Important report, based on a survey carried out in 1957.]

SG.30. 'Gaelic in Highland Schools', in *Transactions of the Gaelic Society of Inverness,* VII (1877-78), 11-18.

[Statistical analysis.]

XVIII. Welsh

W.1. Sir Joseph Bradney, *A Memorandum, being an attempt to give a Chronology of the Decay of the Welsh Language in the Eastern Part of the County of Monmouth,* written at the request of the Departmental Committee on Welsh in connection with the Board of Education, Abergavenny, 1926.

[This work, which I have been unable to consult, is listed (No. 54) in *Dwyieitheg — Bilingualism,* see above, II, *Bibliographies,* Welsh.]

W.2.   T. Darlington, 'The English-speaking Population of Wales', in *Wales*, I (1894), 11-16.
[Historical survey, from the Middle Ages to the 1891 census, of the progressive anglicization of parts of Wales.]

W.3.   T. Darlington, 'Radnorshire and the Welsh Language', in *Wales*, II (1895) 31-32.
[Brief historical survey of the anglicization of Radnorshire from the 16th century onwards.]

W.4.   J. A. Davies, 'The Decline of the Welsh Language in a sample of the Faculty area', in *Bulletin No.* 6, Faculty of Education, University College of Wales, Aberystwyth, 1959, 9-10.

W.5.   Richard E. Davies, *Bilingualism in Wales*, Cape Town/Wynberg/ Johannesburg, 1954, xi-104 pp.
[Deals in particular with the teaching of Welsh in schools and related problems.]

W.6.   A. H. Dodd, 'Welsh and English in East Denbighshire: a Historical Retrospect', in *Transactions of the Honourable Society of Cymmrodorion*, 1940, 34-65.

W.7.   Ll. P. C. Dodd, *A Report on a Language and Cultural Survey of the Schools in Denbighshire*, Denbighshire Education Committee, 1950.

W.8.   A. J. Ellis, 'On the Delimitation of the English and Welsh Languages', in *Y Cymmrodor*, V (1882), 173-208.
[Traces the linguistic divide between Welsh and English in Pembrokeshire and Gower and from Flintshire to Monmouthshire.]

W.9.   S. J. Evans, 'Welsh in Education and Life', in *Welsh Secondary Schools Review*, 13 (1937), 84-89.

W.10.   I. Ll. Foster, 'Bilingualism and the Schools of Wales', in *Blackfriars*, March, 1954, 103-109.

W.11.   R. A. Fowkes, 'English Idiom in Modern Welsh', in *Word*, I (1945), 239-248.
[Examples of the word-for-word translation of English idioms into Welsh.]

W.12.   R. Hindley, *Linguistic Distributions in North East Wales.*
A study in geographical and historical evolution. Unpublished
undergraduate dissertation, University of Leeds Department of
Geography, 1950.
[Includes a separate atlas volume.]

W.13.   R. Hindley, *Linguistic distributions in South East Wales. A study*
in trends over the last century. Unpublished M.A. thesis, University of Leeds, 1962.
[Includes a separate atlas volume.]

W.14.   John Hughes, *The Development of the National Language,*
Literature and History in the Educational System of Wales,
unpublished M.A. thesis, University of Wales, 1922.

W.15.   I. James, *The Welsh Language in the* 16th *and* 17th *Centuries,*
Cardiff, 1887, 49 pp.

W.16.   C. O. Jones, *Yr Iaith Gymraeg ym Mywyd Cyhoeddus Cymru,*
1947, (Undeb Cymru Fydd), 19 pp.
['The Welsh Language in Public Life in Wales'.]

W.17.   E. Jones, 'Welsh-speaking in the New World. I, United States',
in *Lochlann,* I (1958), 241-250.

W.18.   E. Jones and W. R. Owen, 'Welsh-speaking in the New World. II,
Patagonia', in *Lochlann,* I (1958), 251-260.
[Aspects of the situation of the Welsh language in Patagonia
since the founding of the Welsh-speaking colony there in 1865
are discussed in R. Bryn Williams's books on the history of the
colony, *Cymry Patagonia,* Aberystwyth, 1942, 151 pp. and
Y Wladfa, Cardiff, 1962, 334 pp., *passim.*]

W.19.   E. Jones and I. L. Griffiths, 'A Linguistic Map of Wales: 1961',
in *Geographical Journal,* 129 (1963), 192-196.
[Map and commentary based on report of 1961 census.]

W.20.   J. R. Jones, *A raid i'r iaith ein gwahanu?* (Undeb Cymru Fydd),
1967, 26 pp.
['Must the language divide us?']

W.20a. R. Brinley Jones, 'Language and Society in Wales', in *Comparative Education,* 4 (1968), 205-211.

W.21.　T. Gwynn Jones, 'The Present Position and Prospects of the Language and Literature of Wales', in *The Celtic Conference, 1917: Reports*, Perth, 1918, 20-31.

W.22.　W. R. Jones, *Addysg Ddwyieithog yng Nghymru*, Caernarfon, 1963, 141 pp.

['Bilingual Education in Wales'.]

W.23.　W. R. Jones, 'Attitude towards Welsh as a Second Language— a Preliminary Investigation', in *British Journal of Educational Psychology*, XIX (1949), 44-52.

[Analysis of the attitude of pupils aged 11-13+ in a secondary modern school.]

W.24.　W. R. Jones, 'Attitude towards Welsh as a Second Language', in *British Journal of Educational Psychology*, XX (1950), 117-132.

[A more detailed study than in No. 23 above, and based on a different school, of the attitude of pupils aged 11-15.]

W.25.　W. R. Jones, *Bilingualism in Welsh Education*, Cardiff, 1966, xiv-202 pp.

[See particularly Part I, 'The Historical Background', pp. 1-85].

W.25a.　Robyn Lewis, *Second-Class Citizen*, Llandysul, 1969, xix-125 pp.

[A collection of essays designed to show that the provisions of *The Welsh Language Act*, 1967, fall short of the principle of 'equal validity' recommended by the report, *Legal Status of the Welsh Language* (W.83), and to illustrate various aspects of the position of Welsh in public life in the period immediately before and since the act was passed. The text of the act is quoted in full, pp. 122-125.]

W.26.　Saunders Lewis, *Tynged yr Iaith*, 1962, 30 pp. (BBC Welsh Lecture for 1962).

['The Fate of the Language']

W.27.　T. Lewis, 'Sur la distribution du parler gallois dans le Pays de Galles d'après le recensement de 1921', in *Annales de géographie*, XXXV (1926), 413-418.

[Summarized by Vendryes, *Revue Celtique*, 44 (1927), 216-218.]

W.28. W. Llewelyn-Williams, 'The Claims of the Welsh Language', in *Wales*, III (1896), 455-460.

[A protest against the inferior status of Welsh, especially in schools, and a plea for improvement.]

W.29. A. Llywelyn-Williams, 'Welsh in Adult Education and Life Today', in *Adult Education*, 32 (1959-60), 287-290.

[The role of Welsh in adult classes organized by extra-mural departments of the University and by the W.E.A.]

W.30. P. Mocaer, *L'Enseignement bilingue au Pays de Galles* (avec préface de J. Loth), Lorient, 1915, ix-38 pp.

W.31. Dyfnallt Morgan, 'Welsh, a Language in Retreat?' in *The Welsh Anvil*, IV (1952), 64-69.

W.32. Gerald Morgan, *The Dragon's Tongue*, [Rhiwbeina, The Triskel Press], 1966, 144 pp.

[In spite of the flippant title, this book gives a sober and well-documented account of the fortunes of the Welsh language since mediaeval times and of its present-day situation.]

W.33. Ll. Hooson Owen, *A History of the Welsh Language in Radnorshire from 1536*, unpublished M.A. thesis, Liverpool, 1951.

W.34. I. C. Peate, 'The Present State of the Welsh Language', in *Lochlann*, III (1965), 420-431.

W.35. I. C. Peate, 'The Welsh Language as a Medium of Instruction in the University of Wales', in *Lochlann*, I (1958), 261-262.

W.36. H. Pilch, 'Bilinguisme au Pays de Galles', in *Miscelánea Homenaje a André Martinet*, I, 1957, 223-241.

[Stresses the superior prestige of English even amongst Welsh-speakers and the progressive anglicization of Welsh vocabulary and idiom.]

W.37. A. Pinsent, 'A Bilingual Policy for Wales, and how to Achieve it', in *The Welsh Anvil*, 6 (1954), 42-62.

[A review article, based on the report *The Place of Welsh and English in the Schools of Wales*, see below No. 81.]

W.38.   G. Price, 'La situation actuelle de la langue galloise', in *Lo Gai Saber* (Toulouse), No. 292, mars-abrilh, 1960, 201-205.

W.39.   Alwyn D. Rees, *The Magistrate's Dilemma vis-à-vis the Welsh Language Offender*, Llandybie, [1968], 28 pp.

W.40.   Ioan Bowen Rees, 'Welsh and the Professions', in *The Welsh Anvil*, II (1950), 98-101.
[The problems of the many Welsh-speaking people who are well-educated in English but are only semi-literate in Welsh.]

W.41.   W. H. Rees, *The Vicissitudes of the Welsh Language in the Marches of Wales, with special reference to its territorial distribution in modern times*, unpublished Ph.D. thesis, University of Wales, 1947.

W.42.   Sir John Rhys and Sir David Brynmor Jones, *The Welsh People*, London, 1900, xxvi-678 pp. (and various later revised editions).
[Ch. XII, 'Language and Literature', (pp. 501-550) contains a valuable survey of the state of the language at various periods, with numerous facts relating to Welsh in the schools, the state of Welsh publishing, numbers of speakers, etc.]

W.43.   M. Richards, 'Standard and dialect in Welsh', in *Archivum Linguisticum*, II (1950), 46-55.
[A historical survey of the growth and development of the standard literary language from the 12th century onwards, and problems arising from the fact that the standard is not based on any one particular dialect.]

W.44.   S. W. Semple, *The Problem of Bilingualism in the Schools of Wales and Scotland*, Toronto, 1964, vii-47 pp.
[Wales, Part I, pp. 1-23; for comment, v. sup. Scottish Gaelic, No. 16.]

W.45.   M. L. Sjoestedt, 'La littérature qui se fait en Galles', in *Études Celtiques*, IV (1948), 67-82.
[Bibliographical survey of contemporary publications of all kinds in Welsh.]

W.46.   F. Smith, 'Welsh Schools and the Language Problem', in *Welsh Outlook*, IV (1917), 24-27.
[The unsatisfactory nature of the teaching of Welsh in schools and suggestions for improvements.]

W.47.   A. Sommerfelt, 'The Destiny of Welsh', in *Lochlann*, III (1965), 432.

W.48.   J. E. Southall, *Wales and her Language*, Newport and London 1892, 396 pp.
[In spite of the unsound and pretentious "philology" contained in its early chapters, the book is useful for its chapters on the teaching of Welsh in schools, Welsh periodicals and the geographical limits of the language.]

W.49.   J. E. Southall, *The Welsh Language Census of 1891*, Newport, 1895, 58 pp. and a map.

W.50.   J. E. Southall, *The Welsh Language Census of 1901*, Newport, 1904.

W.51.   J. Gareth Thomas, 'The Geographical Distribution of the Welsh Language', in *Geographical Journal*, 122 (1956), 71-79.
[Based on the report on the 1951 census.]

W.52.   J. Gareth Thomas, 'The Welsh Language', in *Wales: a physical, historical and regional geography*, ed. by E. G. Bowen, London, 1957, 247-263.
[Studies the recession of Welsh, its present extent, and factors influencing its fortunes.]

W.53.   T. A. Watkins, 'Background to the Welsh Dialect Survey', in *Lochlann*, II (1962), 38-49.
[Comments on the decline of Welsh as revealed by the 1951 census report; whether or not the present Welsh-language policy in schools succeeds in arresting the decline of Welsh, it is a contributory factor to the disappearance of dialect.]

W.54.   D. T. Williams, 'The Distribution of the Welsh Language, 1931-1951', in *Geographical Journal*, 119 (1953), 331-335.
[Based on an analysis of the reports on the 1931 and 1951 censuses.]

W.55.   D. T. Williams, 'Gower: a Study in Linguistic Movements and Historical Geography', in *Archaeologia Cambrensis*, 89 (1934), 302-327.
[The distribution of Welsh in Gower since 1891 and factors affecting anglicization from the Middle Ages onwards.]

W.56.   D. T. Williams, 'Linguistic Divides in South Wales,' in *Archaeologia Cambrensis*, 90 (1935), 239-266.
[The border between Welsh and English.]

W.57.   D. T. Williams, 'Linguistic Divides in North Wales', in *Archaeologia Cambrensis*, 91 (1936), 194-209.

W.58.   D. T. Williams, 'A Linguistic Map of Wales according to the 1931 Census', in *Geographical Journal*, 89 (1937), 146-151.

W.59.   Ifor Williams, *Cymraeg Byw*, 1960, 26 pp. (BBC Welsh Lecture for 1960).
['Living Welsh'; a plea for bringing the literary language and the spoken language closer together.]

W.60.   James G. Williams, *Mother Tongue and Other Tongue, or a Study in Bilingualism*, Bangor, 1915, viii-116 pp.
[Deals mainly with Belgium and Alsace-Lorraine. N.B. however, Ch.VI, 'Applications to Wales', (a) 'Lessons of the 1911 Census' (pp. 100-103), (b) 'Bilingual Teaching' (pp. 104-116).]

W.61.   J. L. Williams, 'The National Language in the Social Pattern in Wales', in *Studies* (Dublin), 47 (1958), 247-258.

W.62.   J. L. Williams, 'This Bilingual Game', in *The Welsh Anvil*, 8 (1958), 32-40.
[Present methods of implementing a bilingual policy in schools are failing to make the great majority of English-speakers bilingual; suggestions for improvements.]

W.63.   J. L. Williams, 'The Turn of the Tide: Some Thoughts on the Welsh Language in Education', in *Transactions of the Honourable Society of Cymmrodorion*, 1963, Part I, 48-69.

W.64.   S. J. Williams, 'Y Gymraeg a'r Dyfodol', in *Transactions of the Honourable Society of Cymmrodorion*, 1942, 148-157.
['The Welsh Language and the Future.']

W.65.   W. Ogwen Williams, 'The Survival of the Welsh Language after the Union of England and Wales: the First Phase, 1536 - 1642', in *Welsh Historical Review*, II (1964 - 65), 67 - 93.

W.66.   *Census of England and Wales, 1901.*

[In the reports on each of the Welsh counties—published London, 1903, except for the volume on Monmouthshire which appeared in 1902—the figures for Welsh-speakers are given in Table IV. See also No. 50 above.]

W.67.   *Census of England and Wales, 1911*, Vol. XII, *Language Spoken in Wales and Monmouthshire*, London ,1913.

[This excellent idea of publishing the figures for Welsh-speakers in a separate volume instead of distributing them amongst the various county reports was unfortunately abandoned in the reports on the 1921 and 1931 censuses, but taken up again in the reports on the 1951 and 1961 censuses.]

W.68.   *Census of England and Wales, 1921.*

[In the reports on each of the Welsh counties—published London, 1924—the figures for Welsh-speakers are given in Tables 25 and 25a, with a commentary in the Introduction. See also J. Vendryes' summary of the report, 'Statistique de la langue galloise en Galles', in *Revue Celtique*, 43 (1926), 217 - 218, and No. 27 above.]

W.69.   *Census of England and Wales, 1931.*

[In the reports on each of the Welsh counties—published London, 1933,—the figures for Welsh-speakers are given in Tables 17 and 18, with a commentary in the Introduction. See also Nos. 54 and 58 above and F. Wyn Jones, 'Wales and the Census', in *Welsh Outlook*, 20 (1933), 299 - 302.]

W.70.   *Census 1951, Wales (including Monmouthshire). Report on Welsh Speaking Population*, London 1955.

[Apart from the 1911 report—see 67 above—this was the first occasion on which the figures for Welsh-speakers were gathered together in one volume. This report is the subject of a note in *Études Celtiques*, VI (1953 - 54), 206 - 209. See also Nos. 51 and 54 above.]

W.71.   *Census 1961. Wales (including Monmouthshire). Report on Welsh Speaking Population*, London, 1962.
[See also No. 19 above and No. 76 below.]

W.72.   Board of Education, *Welsh in Education and Life*, London, 1927, xx - 346 pp.
[A most useful survey. Part I, pp. 1 - 81, 'Introduction, Historical and general'; Part II, pp. 83 - 179, 'Present Position'; Part III pp. 180 - 306, 'Problems and Lines of Solution.']

W.73.   Caernarvonshire Education Authority, *Ysgolion Sir Gaernarfon: Pedwerydd Arolwg Iaith - Caernarvonshire Schools: Fourth Language Survey*, 1960, 40 pp.
[Covers the use of Welsh in the schools and in the home. The Caernarvonshire Education Authority's first language survey was published in 1944, the second in 1948 and the third in 1952.]

W.74.   Cardiganshire Education Committee, *Welsh Language Survey, 1961*, 1962, 23 pp.
[Information on language surveys in Cardiganshire schools made in 1945, 1949 and 1961. A report of a survey made in 1967 is forthcoming.]

W.75.   Central Advisory Council for Education (Wales), *Primary Education in Wales*, London, 1967, xxxvi - 646 pp.

[See especially Part III, Ch. II. 'Welsh in the Primary Schools', pp. 209 - 256; short sections elsewhere in the volume are also relevant.]

W.76.   The Council for Wales and Monmouthshire, *Report on the Welsh Language Today*, London, 1963, 151 pp.
[This indispensable official report contains a historical introduction, a comprehensive survey of the use of Welsh in government and administration, working life, leisure, religious worship and education, an analysis (with 3 maps) of the results of the 1961 census, and a number of recommendations.]

W.77.   Home Office, *Report of the Committee on Welsh Language Publishing*, London, 1952, 30 pp.
[See also 'Welsh Publishing Today', in *The Times Literary Supplement*, 6 - 5 - 1960, p. 296.]

W.78.   Ministry of Education, 'Welsh and English in Wales.' in *Language, some suggestions for teachers of English and others*, London 1954, pp. 94 - 109.

W.79.   Ministry of Education, Welsh Department, *Bilingualism in the Secondary School in Wales* (Pamphlet No. 4), London, 1949.

W.80.   Ministry of Education, Welsh Department, *Education in Wales, 1847 - 1947: Addysg yng Nghymru, 1847 - 1947*, London, 1948 (reprinted 1957), 48 pp.

W.81.   Ministry of Education, Welsh Department, *The Place of Welsh and English in the Schools of Wales* (Report of the Central Advisory Council for Education [Wales]), London 1953 (reprinted 1960), xii - lll pp. + a map.
         [An important, well-documented report, containing a historical survey, an assessment of the present position, and recommendations for future developments.]

W.82.   Ministry of Education, Welsh Department, *The Place of Welsh and English in the Schools of Wales: Lle'r Gymraeg a'r Saesneg yn Ysgolion Cymru*, London, 1953, vi - 69 pp. + a map.
         [A summary in English and Welsh of No. 81 above.]

W.82a.   Welsh Joint Education Committee, *Language Survey, 1961*, n.p., 28 pp.
         [A follow-up to No. 81 above.]

W.83.   Welsh Office, *Legal Status of the Welsh Language*, London, 1965 vi - 84 pp.
         [A comprehensive survey of the present legal position of Welsh in various fields of activity and recommendations for raising and clarifying the legal status of the language. In particular it is recommended that anything done in Welsh in Wales should have the same legal force as if it had been done in English.]

XIX. Index of Authors

The following abbreviations are used:

Bibl.	:	Bibliographies	Ir.	:	Irish
Gen.	:	General Works	Man.	:	Manx
Ba.	:	Basque	Oc.	:	Occitan
Br.	:	Breton	R.	:	Romansh
Cat.	:	Catalan	Sard.	:	Sardinian
Celt.	:	Celtic Languages	Sc.	:	Scots
Far.	:	Faroese	SG.	:	Scottish Gaelic
Fra.	:	France (general)	W.	:	Welsh
Fri.	:	Frisian			

Aitken, A. J.	Sc.6
Alton, J.	R.1
Altube, Severo de	Ba.1
Amade, J.	Bibl. (Catalan, i); Cat. 1
Amundsen, S.	Bibl. (Faroese, ii); Far. 1
Anderson, C.	Ir.1
Aramon i Serra, R.	Bibl. (Catalan, ii); Cat. 2
Aspey, D.	SG.9 (i)
Aurouze, J.	Fra.1

Badía Margarit, A.	Cat.3, 4, 5, 6
Bähler, E. L.	R.2
Bald, M.	Sc.1
Bannerman, W.	SG.1
Banqué, B.	Cat.7
Battisti, C.	R.3, 4, 5, 6
Baur, A.	R.7
Bebb, W. A.	Br.1
Bergin, O.	Ir.16, 34
Berthaud, P.-L.	Bibl. (Occitan, ii, iii); Fra.15; Oc.1
Berther, F.	R.8
Berthou, G.	Bibl. (Breton, ii.)
Bezzola, R. R.	R.9, 10
Blanc, -	Oc.2
Blanes, A.	Cat.21
Boelens, K.	Fri.1, 2

Bonaparte, Prince Lucien	Ba.2
Bradney, J.	W.1
Breatnach, R. A.	Ir.1a, 2, 46
Brennan, M.	Ir.25b (ii), 46
Bringuier, O.	Oc.18
Broca, P.	Ba.3
Browne, P.	Ir.34
Brummer, R.	Cat.8
Brun, A.	Cat.9; Oc.3, 4, 5
Brunot, F.	Fra.2, 3
Buwalda, H.S.	Bibl. (Frisian, iii)

Caduff, G.	R.11
Cahill, E.	Ir.3, 3a
Campbell, D.	Man.1
Campbell, J. L.	SG.2, 3, 17
Carmody, F. J.	Man.2
Caro Baroja, J.	Ba.4
Catford, J. C.	Sc.2
Cavigelli, P.	R.12
Cluzel, I.-M.	Bibl. (Occitan, iv, v, vi)
Cohen ,G.	Ba.3, 9
Colville, J.	Sc.3
Coogan, T. P.	Ir.3b
Corkery, D.	Ir.4
Coromines, J.	Cat.10
Costes, C.	Oc.6
Craig, D.	Sc.4
Craigie, W.A.	Sc.5, 6
Cubbon, W.	Bibl. (Manx)
Cunnane, J.	Ir.46
Curtis, E.	Ir.4a

Darlington, T.	W.2, 3
Dauzat, A.	Gen.1; Ba.2, 3; Br.2, 3, 4, 21; Fra.4, 11, 12
Davies, A. S. B.	Man.3
Davies, J. A.	W.4
Davies, R. E.	Ir.5; W.5
Decurtins, A.	R.13
del Vecchio, G.	R.36
Demangeon, A.	Ir.5a

Denez, P.	Br.5
Deplazes, G.	R.14
Dodd, A. H.	W.6
Dodd, Ll. P. C.	W.7
Domhnallain, T. O.	Ir.6
Dourguin, C.	Oc.20
Duhamel, G.	Fra.13
Dujardin, L.	Br.10
Dunn, C. W.	SG.4, 9(ii)
Du Scorff, A.	Br.6
Ellis, A. J.	W.8
Elwert, T.	Oc.7
Ernault, E.	Br.7
Evans, D. S.	Ir.7
Evans, S. J.	W.9
Falc'hun, F.	Br.5, 8, 9, 10, 11
Fels, E.	Ir.7a
Fink, P.	R.15
Fleuriot, G.	Ba.5
Fokkema, K.	Bibl. (Frisian, ii); Fri.3, 4, 5, 6, 7, 8
Foppema, Y.	Fri.9
Foster, I. Ll.	W.10
Fouéré, Y.	Br.12, 13
Fowkes, R. A.	W.11
Francescato, G.	R.16, 17
Freeman, T. W.	Ir. 8
Gaidoz, H.	Ir.11; SG.12
Gartner, Th.	R.18, 19
Gautier, M.	Br.14
Gavel, H.	Ba.6; Fra.5
Gieré, G. -R.	R.20
Gourvil, F.	Br.15
Grant, W.	Sc.7, 8
Gray, A.	Sc.9
Gray, T.	Ir.9
Gregg, R. G.	Ir.10
Griera, A.	Bibl. (Catalan, iii, iv, v); Cat.11

Grieve, C. M.	Sc.10 (*see also* MacDiarmid, H.)
Griffiths, I. L.	W.19
Guieysse, M.	Br. 16
Guiter, E.	Cat.12
Haskell, D. C.	Bibl. (Occitan, i)
Heeroma, K.	Fri.10
Hegnauer, C.	R.21
Hemon, R.	Bibl. (Breton, iii); Br.17, 18
Heilmann, L.	R.22
Hellinga, W. G.	Fri.11
Heslinga, M. W.	Ir.11a
Hindley, R.	Celt. 1; W.12, 13
Holmer, N. M.	Ir.12, 13
Hughes, J.	W.14
Humphrey's, H. Ll.	Br.19
Hunter, J.	SG.5
Hyde, D.	Ir.14
Irigaray, A.	Ba.7
Jackson, K. H.	Man.4; SG.6, 9(iii)
James, I.	W.15
Jenner, H.	Celt.4; Man.5
Jones, C.O.	W.16
Jones, D. B.	W.42
Jones, E.	Celt.2; W.17, 18, 19
Jones, F. W.	W.69
Jones, J. R.	W.20
Jones, R. B.	W.20a
Jones, T. G.	W.21
Jones, W. R.	W.22, 23, 24, 25
Jump, J. R.	Ba.8
Kearns, C.	Ir.15
Kéraval, P.	Br.19a
Kinsley, J.	Sc.11
Kloss, H.	Far.2; Fri.12; Sc.12
Kneen, J. J.	Man.6

Kollmann, P.	Fri.13
Krenn, E.	Far. 3
Krogmann, W.	Fri.14
Kuhn, A.	R.23

Lach-Szyrma, W. S.	Man.7
Lacombe, G.	Ba.3, 9
Lafitte, P.	Bibl. (Basque, ii); Ba.10
Lafon, R.	Ba.2, 11
Lafont, R.	Fra.6; Oc.8
Lagarde, P.	Oc.9
Lansel, P.	R.24
Lecuona, M. de	Ba.12
Legris, M.	Fra.7
Lehmacher, G.	Ir.16
Le Quer, A.	Br.20
Lesaffre, J.	Bibl. (Occitan, iii, iv, v, vi); Fra.16; Oc.10
Lewis, R.	W.25a
Lewis, S.	W.26
Lewis ,T.	W.27
Liebeskind, W. A.	R.25
Llewellyn-Williams, W.	W.28
Lloyd, D. M.	Br. 24; Ir.17
Llywelyn-Williams, A.	W.29
Lockwood, W. B.	Far.4, 5; Fri.15
Lorimer, W. L.	SG.7
Loth, J.	Br.21
Lüdtke, H.	R.26

MacDiarmid, H.	Sc.13
(pen-name of Grieve, C. M., *q.v.*)	
MacDonald, K. D.	SG.7a
MacEnri, S. P.	Ir.18
Mackay, G. W.	SG.8
MacLeod, C. I. N.	SG.9
MacLeod, M.	SG.10
Macnamara, J.	Ir.19, 20, 21, 46
MacQueen, L. E. C.	Sc.14
McRae, K. D.	R.27

Marsh, A.	Ir.22
Marteville, A.	Br.24
Martray, J.	Br.22
Matheson, N.	SG.10a
Mauron, C.	Oc.20
Maxfield, M. E.	Bibl. (Romansh, i)
Mayer, K.	R.28
Meiklejohn, M. F. M.	Sard. 1
Meillet, A.	Gen.2; Ba.3, 9
Mescal, J.	Ir.22a
Mocaer, P.	Br.23; W.30
Montoliu, M. de	Cat.13
Moore, A.	Man.8
Moore, A. W.	Man.9
Morf, H.	R.29
Morgan, D.	W.31
Morgan, G.	W.32
Morrison, J. R.	SG.11
Mulcahy, R.	Ir.34
Müller, B.	Oc.11
Murphy, G.	Ir.23
Murray, J. A. H.	Sc.15; SG.12
Myhill, H.	Ba.13

Nisbet, J.	SG.13
Normandy, G.	Cat.14

O Briain, L.	Ir.34
O'Brien, M. C.	Ir.23a
Ó Casaide, S.	Ir.24
O'Connell, F. W.	Ir.16
Ó Cuív, B.	Ir.25, 25a, 25b(i) and (vii)
Ó Danachair, C.	Ir.25b (vi)
O'Dell, A.C.	SG.13a
O'Doherty, E. F.	Ir.26
Ó Fiaich, T.	Ir.25b (v)
O'Flynn, J.	Ir.27
Ogée, J.	Br.24
Ó hAilín, T.	Ir.25b (iv)
Ó Máille, T.	Ir.16

O'Rahilly, T. F.	Ir.16, 28
Ormaechea, N.	Ba.14
Owen, Ll. H.	W.33
Owen, W. R.	W.18
Panier, R.	Br.25
Pansier, P.	Oc.12
Pastre, L.	Cat.15
Paul, H.	Fri.17
Peate, I. C.	W.34, 35
Pellegrini, G. B.	R.30
Perbosc, A.	Fra.8
Peyre, S. -A.	Oc.13
Pilch, H.	W.36
Pinsent, A.	W.37
Pocquet du Haut-Jussé, B.A.	Bibl. (Breton, iv)
Poortinga, Y.	Bibl. (Frisian, iii)
Post, P.	Fri.16
Price, G.	Celt.3; Oc.14; SG.14; W.38
Pult, C.	R.31
Pult, J.	R.32
Ravenstein, E. G.	Celt.4
Rees, A. D.	W.39
Rees, I. B.	W.40
Rees, W. H.	Celt.5; W.41
Rheinfelder, H.	Br.26
Rhys, J.	W.42
Rice, C. C.	Cat.16
Richards, M.	W.43
Ripert, E.	Oc.15
Ross, J.	SG.15
Rostaing, C.	Oc.20
Roumanille, J.	Oc.16
Rouquette, M.	Fra.14
Salvat, J.	Oc.17
Sanna, A.	Sard.2
Sartorious, A.	R.33, 34

Sébillot, P.	Br.25, 27, 28; Celt.4
Semple, S. W.	SG.16; W.44
Sérant, P.	Fra.9
Sheehan, Most Rev. Dr.	Ir.16
Siebs, T.	Fri.17
Sinclair, D. M.	SG.9 (iv)
Sjoestedt [-Jonval], M. L.	Celt.6; Ir.29, 30; W.45
Smith, F.	W.46
Smith, G. G.	Sc.16
Smith, J. A.	SG.16a
Smith, J. C.	Sc.17
Sommerfelt, A.	W.47
Southall, J. E.	Ir.31; W.48, 49, 50

Tauer, N.	Ba.15
Taupiac, J.	Bibl. (Occitan, viii)
Tesnière, L.	Gen.2
Tevenar, G. von	Bibl. (Breton, i); Br.29; Ir.32
Thilo, E.	R.35
Thomas, E. W.	Cat.17
Thomas, J. G.	W.51, 52
Thomson, D. S.	Celt.7
Thomson, G.	Ir.33
Tierney, M.	Ir.34
Torreilles, Ph.	Cat.18
Tourné, M.	Cat.21
Tournier, M.	Ba.16
Tourtoulon, Ch. de	Oc.18
Trépos, P.	Br.11

Vallée, F.	Br.30
Vallverdú, F.	Cat.18a, 21
Varin, P.	Br.24
Veen, J. v. d.	Fri.2
Vendryes, J.	Ir.45; SG.17, 24; W.68
Ventura, J.	Gen. 2a
Veny i Clar, J.	Cat.18b
Véran, J.	Oc.19
Vinson, J.	Bibl. (Basque, i)
Vives, J.	Bibl. (Catalan, ii)

Wagner, G.	Sc.18
Wagner, H.	Ir.34a, 34b
Wagner, M. L.	Sard. 3
Wall, M.	Ir.25b (iii)
Walton, K.	SG.13a
Warrack, A.	Sc.8
Watkins, T. A.	W.53
Watson, W. J.	SG.18, 19
Werner, O.	Bibl. (Faroese, i); Far.6
Widmer, A.	R.12, 37
Williams, D.	Ir.25a
Williams, D. T.	W.54, 55, 56, 57, 58
Williams, I.	W.59
Williams, J. G.	W.60
Williams, J. L.	W.61, 62, 63
Williams, R. B.	W.18
Williams, S. J.	W.64
Williams, W. O.	W.65
Wilson, J.	Sc.19
Woolley, J. S.	Bibl. (Scots; Scottish Gaelic)
Woude, G. v. d.	Fri.18
Wumkes, G. A.	Bibl. (Frisian, i)
Wunderli, P.	R.38
Young, D.	Sc.20, 21, 22
Zeman, K.	Far.7
Zimmer, H.	Br.31; Celt.8